The Lincoln-Kennedy Coincidences

T0197964

The Lincoln-Kennedy Coincidences

Fact and Legend in the Assassinations

JONATHAN KNIGHT

McFarland & Company, Inc., Publishers
Jefferson, North Carolina

ISBN (print) 978-1-4766-9055-1
ISBN (ebook) 978-1-4766-4846-0

Library of Congress and British Library
Cataloguing data are available

Library of Congress Control Number 2022057332

Front cover: (top) colorized photograph of Abraham Lincoln
by Alexander Gardner, 1863 (Library of Congress); (bottom)
photograph of John F. Kennedy by Cecil Stoughton, 1963
(National Archives and Records Administration)

Printed in the United States of America

McFarland & Company, Inc., Publishers
Box 611, Jefferson, North Carolina 28640
www.mcfarlandpub.com

For Julie

"Coincidence is the word we use when we
can't see the levers and pulleys."
—Emma Bull

Table of Contents

Preface

It's estimated that approximately 15,000 books have been written about Abraham Lincoln. In fact, within the lobby of the Ford's Theatre Center for Education and Leadership stands a tower constructed of a sampling of those books. It's made up of roughly 6,800 titles, less than half the total count, and stands at a whopping 34 feet—a truly amazing monument to the amount of thought and research put into the topic.

Believe it or not, the swath of books about John Kennedy is even larger. Upon the fiftieth anniversary of his death in 2013, the *New York Times* estimated the count at nearly 40,000, with a large percentage of that tally dedicated to his assassination.

Put them together and that's well over 50,000 books covering a wide range of angles into both men, their presidencies, and their tragic deaths. Yet there's never been one quite like this.

Even within the subset of books focusing on each president's assassination, this one is distinct. Rather than walking through the compelling stories of those tragic events or exploring the motivations or even conspiratorial possibilities behind them, this book grabs hold of a thread running through both assassinations: the long list of inexplicable similarities and coincidences between the two events. The echoes of each event within the other have fascinated both casual and serious history buffs for more than half a century.

Chapter by chapter, this book delves into that list and its origins while following the general timeline of each assassination—flying at a different altitude than any of the previous books that have approached these subjects. Along the way, it also delves into side stories and subplots that shine a light into unexplored pockets of each assassination and further tie the two together. From the compilation of the initial list to a campfire story of a curse cast upon the American presidency to the mind-bending metaphysical implications of what all these connections might suggest, this book blends serious historical research with a sprinkle of whimsy.

It began as a simple investigation of that list of eerie coincidences, setting out to decipher which ones are true, which aren't, and how likely (or unlikely) those similarities really are. Over time and exploration, it branched out into something much more satisfying and evolved into what you're about to read: a journey along a path filled with colorful people and places making up some truly compelling anecdotes that you won't believe you haven't heard.

The result is a book that will likely feel at once familiar and new, but also totally unlike any of the thousands that have come before.

Prologue:
Running Mates

Like imagining America before the Pledge of Allegiance or the 99-cent cheeseburger, it's hard to picture a time when Abraham Lincoln wasn't considered the nation's signature president. Or a president at all. Or even a candidate.

In November of 1858, Abraham Lincoln wasn't yet the mascot for democracy he is today, photobombing our currency and being portrayed by gangly, goateed actors in Presidents Day furniture store commercials. Technically, he wasn't even an official politician at this stage of the game. He was a former state representative from Illinois who, as a member of the newly formed Republican Party, was challenging Democrat Stephen Douglas for his seat in the United States Senate.

At the time, U.S. senators were selected by each state's legislature rather than by a popular vote, and in that November's election, the Democrats maintained control of the Illinois General Assembly. When the legislature convened the following January, it re-elected Douglas to another six-year term as senator, with the voting running strictly along party lines.

But Lincoln's "defeat" was less remembered than his campaign. It had been defined by a series of articulate and widely discussed debates leading up to the election, labeled—you guessed it—the Lincoln-Douglas debates. He had made an impression on the state that would soon be calling itself the Land of Lincoln, and even more so on the nation as a whole. As the newfound Republican Party gained support across a polarized nation with its anti-slavery platform, Lincoln had become the face of its success—even though he hadn't been successful himself. It was a perverse distinction that would serve as a harbinger for the man who would become perhaps the most celebrated and haunted figure in American history.

What would come next for the rail-splitter from Illinois might seem natural in retrospect, but in the aftermath of those fateful 1858 midterms in which Lincoln's campaign perished, nobody had yet articulated the idea. That is, until four days after the election, when, far from where Lincoln's political battle had been raged, someone did.

Findlay, Ohio, then as now, was a tiny town tucked in the swampy northwest quadrant of the postage stamp-shaped state, some 400 miles from Lincoln's Illinois home. Also then as now, Findlay wasn't exactly considered a cradle for high-minded political thought. Yet it was there that a successful druggist named Israel Green sat down and forecasted the future of America. A loyal member of the new Republican Party and an avid proponent of the anti-slavery cause, Green had watched Lincoln carefully throughout his senatorial campaign and debate appearances—"watched," of course, solely via the delayed and distant printed word in this era more than a century before television would play a role in politics.

Even in Lincoln's defeat, Green saw greatness in this still relatively obscure man yet to turn 50. And he decided to write a letter to the *Cincinnati Daily Gazette*—a Republican-leaning newspaper he read faithfully—to share his opinion.

"Permit a daily reader of your valuable paper, residing in the Northwest," he began, "to suggest to the consideration of the triumphant and united opposition, the names of the following distinguished and patriotic statesmen as standard bearers in the approaching presidential election."

Beneath, he made the first suggestion that this up-and-coming Abraham Lincoln should run for president. At the same time, he also proposed another name as his running mate that today sounds much more familiar than it would have at the time. "There, sir," he stated matter-of-factly to the editor of the paper, "is a ticket that can command and receive the united support of the entire opposition."

He ticked off all the wonderful things Lincoln and his

hypothetical vice president would do. Their primary objective would be outlawing slavery in the newly created states, or, as Green put it, "humbug squatter sovereignty," while ensuring a "return to the early principles and practices of the founders of our government." After his laundry list of reasons outlining how Lincoln and his running mate would change the country for the better, Green confidently concluded: "With such standard bearers and such a platform, the great opposition or American Republican Party can go before the people of the nation in 1860 with the full assurance of a triumphant victory over the present pro-slavery filibustering, border ruffian Democracy."

Green's letter, published in the *Gazette* on November 10, was the starting gun. Other newspapers and politicians took up the idea, and Lincoln quickly became a serious contender for the Republican presidential nomination. And we were off to the races toward America as we know it: an iconic presidency ultimately followed by breakdancing Lincoln look-a-likes selling couches over a holiday weekend in February.

As if Green were karmically rewarded for his historic suggestion, the same year Lincoln was elected president, Green was elected mayor of Findlay. At a celebratory rally held in front of the Findlay courthouse after Lincoln's victory, a prominent local attorney spoke to the crowd and brought it all back to Green. "And what could be more appropriate," the attorney declared in a bit of biblical wordplay, "than that Israel should nominate Abraham." A burst of wild applause followed for Findlay's new mayor, who had, after all, tipped over the first domino two years earlier.

Green's recommendation for Lincoln's running mate also garnered consideration and conversation, but ultimately went nowhere. Like Lincoln, Green's suggested vice presidential candidate was anti-slavery and had a thin political resume, having served one term in the Maryland House and then less than a year as secretary of the Navy. Were it not for Green's suggestion that tied him to Lincoln in the embryonic stages of Lincoln's rise to American sainthood, this gentleman, who wound up dying shortly after Lincoln did, would likely be lost to history.

But his name would not.

For on that November day all those years ago, the eerily prescient druggist from the backwoods of Ohio had suggested a presidential ticket consisting of two names that would echo eerily through the corridors of American history.

Abraham Lincoln and John Kennedy.

1

A Fascinating List
of Apparent Nonsense

I don't remember exactly where it happened.

Probably in a museum gift shop. That's always been a spot to which young children are drawn to try to salvage some sort of meaning (and, if they play their cards right, some sort of candy) out of a long—and let's not kid ourselves, at that age, often boring—trip to a dusty old building filled with broken and/or dead things.

Best guess, I was probably about eleven, in the prime of my youth, basking in the elementary glory of, let's say, fifth grade. I was killing time, waiting for my parents or sister or field-trip classmates in the strategically placed bunker of capitalism that you'll find in the generally nonprofit institutions of learning that litter a culture that tends to be indifferent to its own history. While the salient details of the discovery are, as I say, a bit sketch, I remember the feeling quite clearly. Like a lightning bolt sizzling through my 71-pound (or maybe 82-pound) body.

Right there, hanging on the wall—or perhaps in one of those hinged frame-turner deals with which you can leaf through different posters—was an eleven-by-fourteen introduction to a genuine mystery of American history.

To its credit, its bold headline ended with a question mark, framing its thesis as merely a possibility, not a declaration. Still, printed on a thick parchment deliberately made to look wrinkled, aged, and important, it looked just like the other replicas hanging beside it: namely, the Declaration of Independence, the Bill of Rights, the Emancipation Proclamation, and the Gettysburg Address. Add to that the historically accurate reproductions of Civil War currencies

Left: Abraham Lincoln, the first U.S. president to be assassinated (Library of Congress). *Right:* John Fitzgerald Kennedy, the fourth U.S. president to be assassinated (Library of Congress).

and maps that looked like they were taken straight off Ulysses Grant's whiskey-stained living room wall, and this poster with the question mark headline bore a bit more weight. Call it legitimacy by association.

"Lincoln-Kennedy Coincidence?" it ruminated in thick black ink across the top, bookended by images of, no surprise, presidential order number 16 and number 35: Abraham Lincoln and John Kennedy. Beneath the headline, the poster ticked off eighteen overlapping or similar details that connected both the assassinations of the two presidents and the presidents themselves.

At first glance, my eleven- or possibly twelve-year-old self stood there slack-jawed, taking in the list and burrowing its details deep down into my long-term memory. It was genuinely one of the most fascinating things I'd ever seen. That isn't saying much for someone who still didn't have cable television, but that statement still holds true today. And that's exactly what the creator of the poster was going for.

Like the discovery of cheese and penicillin, it was an enterprise inspired by clumsiness. In 1926, a Philadelphia druggist named Charles Promislo accidentally spilled a beaker of chemicals on his lab table, and it soaked into the papers spread across it. When he returned the next morning, he saw that the chemicals had caused a unique reaction. Rather than just becoming flimsy as if doused with water, the papers had taken on a new personality: wrinkled, aged, and old. Or, in the right context, *authentic*.

A history buff, Promislo was fascinated by the transformation and saw a way to run with it. He spent years perfecting the process that had begun with that spilled beaker, eventually settling on an eleven-step recipe for creating perfectly authentic-looking replicas of important historical documents. He founded the Historical Documents Company and first began selling his artificially aged documents at the 1939 World's Fair in New York. He kept adding to the catalog over the years and grew the business, which is still in the family. Today the Historical Documents Company offers more than 500 items in its catalog—from a 1744 listing of the original rules of golf to a reproduction of a wanted poster for Billy the Kid—primarily distributing them to museums and historical sites to sell in their gift shops.

The company has been producing the Lincoln-Kennedy poster for nearly a half century. At times over the years, it's been one of its top sellers. "We had some customers who had an interest in offering it, so we made it," says Alan Weiss, Promislo's grandson, who helps run the company with his family. "It was just intended to be, and still is intended to be, entertaining."

Yet for as entertaining as the content of the poster was, that wasn't what sealed the deal for me, and Weiss explained why. "The idea of having an authentic-looking replica is fairly timeless," he says. "What we're selling isn't just the item, it's the antique parchment paper. That's really the crux of it because people like that so much. Anybody can take the Declaration of Independence and print it on a plain piece of paper. But to actually have a piece in your hands that's printed on parchment and looks and feels old is a different experience."

In fact, some of the items printed by the Historical Documents

Company really have no logical reason to be on parchment. Martin Luther King's "I Have a Dream" speech was added to the roster in recent years, along with JFK's inaugural address—both of which were written and delivered long after the use of parchment. Yet putting them on thick, wrinkled paper makes them even more powerful. And that was, without question, a big part of what drew me to that poster in the first place.

Even without the nod to authenticity to grease the wheels of interest, at eleven or twelve (or maybe even ten, now that I think about it), I knew a little something about odds and the likelihood of coincidence. A very little something, as it happened, but even at that age, I knew that for there to be this many coincidences suggested the possibility that none of it was actually coincidence. And with the lot of them tacked up right there next to the Magna Carta, I knew then and there that this artificially aged sucker had to be on the money.

In retrospect, that was probably the moment I became mesmerized by both of these events in one fell swoop. Sort of a 6–4–3 double play of historical obsession. In the years that followed, with all the historically slanted term papers and book reports I wrote, books and articles I read, and movies and documentaries I watched, my fascination with the Lincoln and Kennedy assassinations began in that moment—when I became convinced that they were somehow cosmically connected.

Which isn't to say that they definitely are. Or that they definitely aren't.

This list of coincidences has been, depending on your source material, both shortened and expanded upon over the years. But since for me (and doubtless many others), this poster is where it all began, let's use this list of eighteen delicious details as the starting point. From here we'll boil off and add onto, expand and redefine and try to whip up a batch of clarity from this recipe of apparent nonsense. We'll account for the naysayers naysaying (warranted and unwarranted), weed out the mistakes and misconceptions, and proceed with a much stronger, more durable list.

Though as we back out of the driveway, a fair warning: along this journey we'll pull over for strange subplots, take random exit ramps through bizarre sidebars, and glide into roadside drive-thrus for a few McNugget-sized tales of curious coincidence.

So here we go, starting with our leadoff hitter on the faux parchment list:

1. Both Lincoln and Kennedy were concerned with civil rights.

At first glance, you can see why this was added, and maybe even why it was put at the top of the list. To be sure, civil rights amounted to a huge topic during both men's time as president. For Lincoln, of course, the country was literally being torn apart over the issue of slavery. And JFK served his term during perhaps *the* defining decade for civil rights in America.

The framework isn't the issue. The big problem with this one is the word "concerned."

It's easy to paint them both as progressive reformers, dedicated to championing the oppressed African American population and ensuring they received fair treatment and equal rights. But that's perhaps a bit of a broad stroke. Lincoln did campaign against slavery and ultimately abolished it with the Emancipation Proclamation and the Thirteenth Amendment to the U.S. Constitution, and he deserves tremendous and due credit for both.

It's a bit more wobbly with Kennedy. It certainly wasn't a major campaign issue in 1960 when he ran for president. You could say he became more tuned in with the issue as his term went on—forced to deal with the riots at the University of Mississippi in 1962 when an African American student named James Meredith had the temerity to enroll, for example.

But "concerned"? On some level, sure. But concerned enough that it would be part of his legacy? It was Lyndon Johnson who pushed the Civil Rights Act through Congress in 1964 after Kennedy's death, leveraging what goodwill and sympathy he could in the months following the assassination to pass a sweeping legislative initiative. JFK had proposed the bill five months before his death, but it had stalled in the Senate like a lawnmower on the first day of spring.

Would Kennedy have picked up the torch anew in his second term and driven it to reality? Or was it his death that ultimately gave it life? We'll never know for sure. But that uncertainty lends weight to this coincidence and makes it a valid opening salvo.

2. Lincoln was elected president in 1860; Kennedy in 1960.

Obviously, there's no interpretation or justification needed on this one. The pair was elected to the White House exactly a century apart. In and of itself, it's no big deal. The four-year presidential election cycle ensures that each election will align with another exactly 100 years earlier. So Dwight Eisenhower, elected in 1952, is similarly connected to Franklin Pierce, elected in 1852.

But, of course, neither of those two was shot and killed.

If you line up the presidents by century and compare those exactly 25 election cycles apart, there's little that jumps out at you in terms of similarities between presidents, either in defining characteristics or administrative legacy.

For instance, let's take a look at the only other two assassinated presidents—James Garfield and William McKinley (whom we'll be bringing up quite a bit as a comparison point for several of the topics on this list). Garfield was elected in 1880, followed by McKinley in 1896, who was then re-elected in 1900. McKinley has Thomas Jefferson 100 years behind him and Bill Clinton 100 years ahead. Obviously, not much connection on either side.

If you really want to be ambitious, you can tie Garfield to Ronald Reagan, first elected in 1980 and shot just a few months into his term, just as Garfield was. Except, of course, Reagan survived. And while it's very possible that Garfield may have survived his shooting as well were it not for some questionable medical decisions made in the weeks following, that's a thin string.

If you want to strain the parameters to the breaking point, you could tie William Henry Harrison (elected in 1840) to Franklin Roosevelt (re-elected for the second time in 1940), since both are members of the elite group of eight presidents to die while in office. But since Roosevelt didn't actually perish until the term *after* this one, the gee-whiz factor sort of dies on the vine.

Point is, you can write off the 100-year connection as not much more than the mathematical equivalent of a rhyme. But since no two presidents elected a century apart have any comparable connection or legacy, either in life or death, it sticks.

3. Both were slain on a Friday and in the presence of their wives.

Again, take it for what you will, but there's no question about the accuracy of this one.

In and of itself, the day-of-the-week similarity isn't huge, though a one-in-seven coincidence seems like less than good odds. (Unless you care to posit that Friday is indeed a much more likely day for a president to be shot. And if so, I'd love to kick my feet up with a beer in my hand and hear that argument.) Garfield and McKinley were also both shot on the same day of the week, a Saturday (perhaps it's a weekend thing?), though neither was with his wife, nor any other corresponding bystanders.

Another coincidence between the timing of the Lincoln and Kennedy assassinations that doesn't make the list but has subsequently been added as a notable sub-point were their proximities to holidays: Lincoln's the Friday before Easter, Kennedy's the Friday before Thanksgiving. So again, if one cares to suggest an assassination tendency toward major holidays, I'm all ears. Otherwise, there's enough meat on the bone to consider this a worthwhile addition to the list.

4. Both were shot from behind and in the head.

The distances of the lethal shots fired varied quite a bit—Lincoln at point-blank range, Kennedy from about a football field away—but the positioning and ultimate impact point were the same. In fact, the entry points for each president's head wound were extremely similar—Lincoln just to the left of center at the base of his skull, Kennedy maybe two inches higher diagonally to the right.

Going back to our assassinated presidents control group, Garfield was also shot from behind from a close distance, in the back, and McKinley was shot at point-blank range from the front. The shots hit them on different sides of their bodies, but from the shooters' perspectives both bullets hit just to the right of the rib cage (facing Garfield's back and McKinley's stomach).

Throw in Reagan's gunshot wound on his side, and that's three other presidents who were shot, but not in the head, and two shot from the front.

5. Their successors, both named Johnson, were southern Democrats, and both were in the Senate.

Here's where it starts to get really interesting.

According to the 2000 U.S. census, Johnson was the second-most common last name in the United States. So you could argue it's not all that huge a coincidence to have a pair of vice presidents with the same last name.

Yet, for as common a name as it is, other than these two, there have been no other "Johnsons" elected as either president or vice president. And aside from the pairs that were related (the Adamses, Roosevelts, and Bushes), no other two presidents have had the same last name.

Just these two.

Perhaps more notable as a coincidence is that they were both Democrats. Not surprising for Kennedy, since he was a Democrat and chose Lyndon Johnson as his running mate in 1960. But Lincoln was a Republican, not a Democrat. As Lincoln was running for re-election in 1864, the Republican Party (which, back then, ultimately decided a candidate's running mate rather than the candidate himself) selected Andrew Johnson, a Democrat, to demonstrate a need for unity. It was a noble and appropriate sentiment, with the nation in the midst of the Civil War. Yet something that hasn't happened since.

They were Southerners: Andrew from Tennessee, Lyndon from Texas (which, while also considered a western state, has generally been lumped into the southern region—for its similar beliefs and characteristics, if nothing else). Lyndon was only the third vice president of the twentieth century from the South, but Andrew had been the latest in a fairly consistent line of Southern VPs (five of the previous ten).

And yes, both came from the Senate, which in and of itself wasn't that unusual. In 1865, eight of the previous ten vice presidents had either served in the Senate at the time of their election to vice president or had served earlier in their career. And Lyndon Johnson was the fourth consecutive elected vice president to rise directly from the Senate. So the Johnson & Johnson senatorial connection was a coincidence, yes, but not a huge one.

That comes next.

6. Andrew Johnson was born in 1808 and Lyndon Johnson was born in 1908.

Sure, you could argue that any two vice presidential candidates would be roughly the same age at the point in their careers they became vice president. Statistically speaking, most are. But this is a conspicuous specificity worthy of note.

Only one other time were two vice presidents elected 100 years apart also born 100 years apart: John Adams, re-elected vice president in 1792, was born in 1735, while Adlai Stevenson (father of the Adlai who would lose two presidential elections to Eisenhower in the 1950s) was born in 1835 and was Grover Cleveland's vice president following the 1892 election.

7. John Wilkes Booth was born in 1839 and Lee Harvey Oswald was born in 1939.

Here's where we have to throw our first flag on the field.

If it sounds a little too good to be true for the men who replaced Lincoln and Kennedy as president as well as the men who removed them from office to all be born exactly 100 years apart, it is. Lee Harvey Oswald was indeed born in 1939, but it turns out that John Wilkes Booth was born in 1838, not, as framed here, exactly a century before Oswald. To be fair, 1839 was cited as Booth's date of birth for decades until later research proved it to be incorrect.

Nevertheless, this is the one entry on the list that can be safely and unquestionably tossed aside.

8. Booth and Oswald were Southerners favoring unpopular ideas.

Technically, you could argue any presidential assassin or would-be assassin favors "unpopular" ideas (first and foremost, of course, being killing the president). So from the outset, this is a pretty thin string connecting Booth and Oswald. But it's still a relatively fair point, since both held beliefs that motivated their decisions.

They did have strong political views—Booth was a white supremacist who was anti–Union and believed deeply in the Confederacy. Oswald was a communist who disagreed with most of the primary tenants of capitalism that fueled the United States' socio-economic engine. While Booth's murder of Lincoln felt much more personal—he despised Lincoln and everything he stood for—Oswald never really had any specific beef against JFK (particularly since most of Kennedy's detractors labeled him as soft on communism). His was more an attack on the system itself than on Kennedy or what he believed in.

And you can't tie Garfield and McKinley's assassins with a similar bow. While Leon Czolgosz's shooting of William McKinley was politically motivated—he was an anarchist lashing out at America's wealthy upper crust in defense of the common working man—it didn't carry the practical (if unrealistic) hope that Booth's shooting of Lincoln did, that it would revive the Southern cause. And of course, Charles Guiteau was the undeniably crazy member of the assassin's quartet, shooting James Garfield because he believed he was denied a well-deserved job in Garfield's new administration.

Similar to the Johnson-Johnson geographical connection, it's fair to label both Booth and Oswald as Southerners. Booth was a Virginian through and through. Oswald did spend about two years growing up in New York City, but was born in New Orleans and spent the bulk of his life living in either Louisiana or Texas.

9. Both presidents' wives lost children through death while in the White House.

Once we get past the grammatical speed bump that is the "through death" phrase (which, via this slightly awkward sentence structure, is required, lest we think they misplaced a child in the Rose Garden and were subsequently unable to find them), this is another coincidence that can't be denied.

Losing a child wasn't all that unusual in Lincoln's time. The Lincolns buried two children, with the latter, Willie, passing away of typhoid fever in 1862 a year into Lincoln's presidency. John and Jackie Kennedy also lost two children: their first child was stillborn in 1956 when Kennedy was a senator, and their son Patrick died of respiratory problems two days after a premature birth, just three months before Kennedy was assassinated.

Though a total of nineteen U.S. presidents lost a child at some point in their lives (in and of itself a surprisingly high number), only one other than Lincoln and Kennedy suffered the loss while president: Calvin Coolidge's teenage son died in 1924 of blood poisoning from a blister on his toe. Just barely missing the list, Grover Cleveland and his wife lost a child in the four-year gap between his two presidential terms.

So here again, a mind-blowing coincidence? No. One that carries some weight? Yes, especially in confluence with the other unusual similarities on the list. Definitely a notable entry.

10. Lincoln's secretary, whose name was Kennedy, advised him not to go to the theatre.

This one, as part of two-step with the next, takes one notable detail and stretches it much too far.

There is no record of Abraham Lincoln ever having a secretary named Kennedy. His two White House secretaries at the time of his death were John G. Nicolay and John Hay. Lincoln was warned (or perhaps "discouraged" would be the better word) from going to the theatre that night by Secretary of War Edwin Stanton for security purposes, even with the war over.

With a similarity in cadence to the next entry on the list, the origin of this coincidence actually had some merit, but was eventually modified past the point of acceptance.

11. Kennedy's secretary, whose name was Lincoln, advised him not to go to Dallas.

John Kennedy did indeed have a secretary named Evelyn Lincoln, who had served in that role since Kennedy joined the U.S.

Senate in 1953. Which, in and of itself, is at least mildly interesting in the context of this discussion. But there's absolutely no evidence of her suggesting that JFK skip the trip to Dallas for any reason.

These two listings are generally the first thing that critics pounce on to undermine the voracity of the swath of coincidences. Unfortunately, they serve little purpose other than to taint the entire list.

12. John Wilkes Booth shot Lincoln in a theatre and ran to a warehouse.

Once again, this one and the next go together, and while still a bit wobbly, has a little more merit. The first part is unquestionably true, the second unquestionably not. Booth shot Lincoln at Ford's Theatre (located at 511 Tenth Street) and then was ultimately surrounded by federal troops in a barn. While in an extremely basic way, a barn is similar to a warehouse in terms of size and philosophy, the two really could not nor should not ever be synonyms.

Not for nothing, Booth also didn't "run" anywhere except to his horse bridled outside the theatre. His primary mode of transportation along his escape route was by horse, along with a frustrating night in a rowboat along the Chesapeake River. And by the time he made it to the barn/warehouse, twelve days had passed, so the inference that he "ran" anywhere directly is another misnomer.

The problematic sentence structure and word choice are conceived solely to connect this entry to the next.

13. Lee Harvey Oswald shot Kennedy from a warehouse and ran to a theater.

This one, on the other hand, is fundamentally correct. It's fair to categorize the Texas School Book Depository (located at 411 Elm Street) as a warehouse since that's in essence what the majority of the building was. And while it was a movie theater rather than a stage theatre that Oswald was eventually arrested in, that's the glue that holds this particular parallel together.

Plus, outside of an interrupted attempt at a bus ride followed by a short journey via taxi to his rooming house, Oswald actually traveled farther on foot than Booth did, stopping just long enough to murder Dallas police officer J.D. Tippit on his way to getting caught at the Texas Theatre.

14. The names Lincoln and Kennedy each contain seven letters.

This is another one you can tear down fairly easily if you want to.

If you divvy up all the U.S. presidents into buckets based on the number of letters in their last names, you'd have seven buckets, each with a varying number of presidents' names within it. While the seven-letter name bucket isn't the fullest (that honor is shared by the five- and six-letter buckets, each with nine presidents), it's tied with eight letters for second place. Six other presidents also have seven letters in their last name, making a total of eight presidents, or roughly seventeen percent. So if you were to randomly draw two presidents' names out of a hat, there's about a one in five chance they'd both have seven letters in their name. And in a broader sense, the odds are minuscule that two presidents' letter counts would match when drawn from a hat, no matter how many letters were in their last names.

Of all the number groupings, the ten-letter club is the only one with just two members: Washington and Eisenhower. But again, using this as a random sampling to compare disparate presidents, what major administrative or life events connect those two?

15. The names Andrew Johnson and Lyndon Johnson each contain thirteen letters.

More or less a sub-point to the Johnson/Johnson parallel in No. 5 and the Lincoln/Kennedy number count in No. 14, this point takes both just a bit further.

Obviously, with the same last name—also making them two of the ten vice presidents with seven-letter last names—they were already more than halfway there to having the same number of letters in their full names. And thus become two of the seven vice presidents whose first and last names combine to thirteen letters—which is the third-highest bucket, trailing only twelve letters (eight) and fourteen letters (ten).

For what it's worth, Chester Arthur, who succeeded James Garfield, also brings thirteen letters to the table, while Theodore Roosevelt buries the needle with the highest tally of all at seventeen letters. And also for what it's worth, of the four other vice presidents who succeeded presidents who died in office, none of them have the same number of letters in their full names—though Millard Fillmore (who replaced Zachary Taylor) and Calvin Coolidge (who replaced Warren Harding) each had eight letters in their last names.

16. The names John Wilkes Booth and Lee Harvey Oswald each contain fifteen letters.

Just one more exploration about letter counts and we'll call it a day. And actually, the primary topic here is less about numbers of letters than it is about middle names.

While both of these murderers have gone down in history by the full, triple-cadence names listed above, neither was known by his full name prior to the respective assassination. Booth was a successful actor from a family of successful actors, and was often referred to simply as "John Wilkes" to distinguish him from his father and brothers. Oswald, conversely, essentially never used his middle name and was known to acquaintances and family as simply "Lee Oswald." The "Harvey" was introduced to his identity the moment he became a suspect in the assassination. Likely because the media initially reported his full name as a formal entry on a police report, it was picked up and repeated so many times that we now can't think of him any other way.

So right away, it's easy to dismiss this one. The letter tally only syncs up when you throw their full names into the mix, and without question, neither went by his full name. But on the other hand, this detail wasn't stretched for inclusion in this list. It's history that made the call to refer to Booth and Oswald by their full names. Therefore making the letter tally fair game rather than logic-straining.

Unlike Lincoln/Kennedy and Johnson/Johnson, neither Booth nor Oswald have the same number of letters in either their first or last names. And for comparison's sake, neither do our other presidential assassins: Charles Guiteau (fourteen) and Leon Czolgosz (twelve).

We could discuss the commonality or lack thereof in number totals in first and last names all day (and who wouldn't want to do that?). But name-length similarity is less notable as an individual point than that it comes up on three different levels. The assassins, the assassinated, and their heirs are all connected by this otherwise ephemeral type of detail. And, while noting valid quibbles about commonality in the dimensions of American names, that's what makes these entries worthy additions to the list.

17. Both assassins were killed before being brought to trial.

Unfortunately, our modern understanding of wackadoodle psychopaths tends to undermine this similarity at first glance. But let us, just for a moment, reflect upon a simpler time when high-stakes murderers truly did intend to get away with their crimes and not perish as a misunderstood martyr in the proverbial flames of knucklehead self-destruction.

Booth—whom, as we'll see, initially hatched a plan to kidnap Lincoln and ransom him rather than kill him—fully intended to make a clean getaway. Even in the throes of his depression in that week after the Confederacy officially surrendered, he never saw his trip to the theatre as a suicide mission. He planned on escaping to his beloved South and being embraced as a hero. He'd be spirited away somewhere deep in the heart of Dixie, where the sanctimonious tentacles of Yankee justice would never be able to find him. To die lying on the front porch of a complete stranger's farmhouse, paralyzed from a shot in the dark fired by a clown-shoes Union soldier was not the final scene he visualized his end credits rolling over.

Similarly, while the full extent of Lee Harvey Oswald's cockamamie postgame plan has never been entirely clear, it's evident that he too never had any intention of going down with his preposterous ship. And even for his final 45 hours or so after being caught, he seemed to revel in all the attention he was getting, even as he denied every charge brought against him. The trial that lay ahead likely would have been the moment he'd been waiting his whole life for.

Thus, for both assassins to be captured but then killed—not in a

Bonnie-and-Clyde-style showdown, but rather each by a totally random wild-card entry into the fray—is, in and of itself, an amazing coincidence that we have never seen before or since.

Conversely, Czolgosz and Guiteau, while not exactly adopting a kamikaze mentality, never seemed to have any intention of getting away with the crime they committed. Each was easily apprehended at the scene, then ultimately brought to trial and summarily executed. Wham, bam, thank you, ma'am—just as you would expect. Just as we would absolutely expect anyone attempting to commit a high-profile political murder today to be killed instantly on the spot, whether successful or not. No trials or manhunts, just a monsoon of protective gunfire from a phalanx of well-armed bodyguards whose sole purpose is this exactly.

We'll delve more deeply into the eerily similar Chutes and Ladders paths both Booth and Oswald took between assassination and their respective demises later. But for now, just the notion that neither would see the inside of a courtroom after being successfully tracked down by authorities is undeniably of note and will forever tie the assassinations together with a clean narrative twine.

18. Both Johnsons were opposed for re-election by men whose names start with "G."

It's a shame we need to close out the list with such an abrupt, record-scratch of a detail (that also turns out to be undeniably wrong), but let's get into it.

Less than a year after Lyndon Johnson assumed the presidency, he ran for election (technically not re-election, since he wasn't elected to the office) against Republican challenger Barry Goldwater. Ninety-six years earlier, Andrew Johnson was replaced as president by Ulysses S. Grant which, presumably, is the G connection referred to here.

But, aside from looking at it in a philosophical sense, Grant never "opposed" Andrew Johnson. Remember, Johnson was a Democrat selected to join Lincoln on the 1864 Republican ticket. As his troubled, impeachment-riddled presidency limped to its conclusion, he entered the fray for the Democratic, not Republican, nomination.

He never really had a chance, and former New York Governor Horatio Seymour won the nomination to face Grant, the Republican nominee, in the 1868 presidential election. Nor did Andrew Johnson face any G names in the battle for the Democratic nomination, unless you count former Ohio representative George Pendleton, which you absolutely should not.

In reality, the likely reason this entry turned out the way it did stemmed from the origin of the list itself (which we'll dive into in greater detail later) just prior to the 1964 election. One of the original entries on the list pointed out that Andrew Johnson was replaced as president by a man whose last name started with G—suggesting that another coincidence may be brewing with the potential of Barry Goldwater winning the '64 election. Of course, Goldwater was routed, and the possibility of a quick, clean coincidence went out the window. Rather than cutting it altogether, the language was changed (how and when we'll get to shortly) from "replaced" to "opposed for re-election," which opened the door to abject erroneousness.

This one, much like Booth's incorrect birth year and Lincoln's imaginary secretary, can be safely removed.

So if you're keeping score at home, that's ten of the eighteen coincidences that are undeniably true, five that are at least partially true, and three that are completely incorrect. We can quibble over how meaningful the certified coincidences are. But while the burden of proof of some sort of mystical connection between the two assassinations lies with those who believe, it then becomes the responsibility of the naysayers to find another similar pattern between a pair of historical figures or events with which they can debunk the uniqueness of Lincoln-Kennedy. And then also write *that* one off as random coincidence.

At the end of the day, the list is like a Rorschach ink blot—different people will see different things. Depending on who you ask, these coincidences could either be a peephole into another dimension or a tale told by an idiot, full of sound and fury and signifying nothing. More likely, it's something in between.

Again going back to the faux historical-looking document that launched these thousand ships, it's important to note that the headline on the poster was a question, not a statement: "Lincoln-Kennedy Coincidence?" It's an escape hatch for anyone who wants to bail out. And if you do, no hard feelings. Godspeed on your departure out of the Neighborhood of Make-Believe and back into the logical, wonder-less world where everything makes sense and nothing connects to anything else.

For those of you still here, let's light a torch. Let's follow this map and see where it takes us.

Personally, after 35 (or maybe 33) years of consideration, I think it's time, if not to find the answer, then at least to partake in a more thorough investigation of the question.

And it seems only fitting that the first step in this journey that has fascinated and mystified so many leads us to a human enigma—a mind-bending genius so next-level brilliant he had to adopt a second personality in an attempt to help us understand him and the way his brain worked.

We begin by stepping into the mysterious world created by Dr. Matrix.

2

The Mystery of Dr. Matrix

"It is naive to suppose that there is such a thing as a randomly arranged group of symbols. Random means without order or pattern.... In my opinion every pattern of symbols conceals a secret meaning, though it may require great skill to discover it."

Those are the words of Dr. Irving Matrix, who claimed to be the reincarnation of Pythagoras and the greatest numerologist in history. And in case you're part of the vast majority which isn't familiar with exactly what that means, numerology, by definition, is the study of the mystical significance of numbers. It's a school of thought that goes back to the ancient Greeks and Hebrew cabalists. Dr. Matrix claimed that no one in history was better at it than him. He may have been right. Almost certainly none was more interesting.

He was born Irving Joshua Bush on a Japanese island in 1908, the son of a reverend from Arkansas leading a Seventh-Day Adventist mission in Kagoshima. Drawn into the world of magic at an early age, he was performing tricks at four years old, then juggling by five. By age eight, as he developed a natural inclination toward numbers, his curiosity began to expand into studying numerical patterns he discovered in the Bible. Eventually coming to the conclusion he didn't adhere to his family's stout religious beliefs, he ran away from home at thirteen and wound up in Tokyo. There he survived on donations collected for the magic tricks he'd perform on the street. He was hired as a magician's assistant, then branched out on his own, traveling through Japan with a mind-reading act while adopting the stage name "Dr. Matrix." It was a moniker he would maintain for the rest of his life.

And what a life it was. After World War II, he moved to Paris and built a burgeoning reputation as an astrologer. Inherently intelligent, he had no official education beyond the sixth grade. Yet he managed to leverage his numerical mysticism into a long line of enterprises, some successful, some not. He became a leading authority on number and language "coincidences," though admitted that they were anything but.

He supported, for example, the theory introduced by previous numerologists that Shakespeare secretly wrote part of the King James translation of the Bible. This belief was based in part on a three-way alignment of details: the 46th word of Psalms 46 was "shake," the 46th word from the end of the psalm was "spear." And the Bard had supposedly completed the work in 1610 when he was— wait for it—46 years old. The key to unlocking this secret, as Dr. Matrix would explain, lies in Shakespeare being born and dying on the same calendar date: April 23. Double 23, you get 46, and you're off to the races.

Correctly interpreted, Dr. Matrix also explained, pi (as in 3.14) conveys the entire history of the human race (which will doubtless come as a relief to all the seventh graders out there wondering why they're being forced to learn about this incomprehensibly important number that just … won't … end).

Dr. Matrix gradually built a reputation as a numerical consultant, or, more in tune with what mere mortals could understand, an astrologer. He could, for example, make predictions on political elections based on the number of letters and numbers in candidates' names. It was rumored, in fact, that French president Charles de Gaulle once sought out his advice. But he was a hard man to track down.

He moved from Paris to New York to Los Angeles to Chicago, but struggled to stay afloat financially. He was arrested for producing counterfeit $20 bills and sentenced to five years in prison, but continued to run his numerology business by mail. Released after just two years for model behavior (or, whispers suggested, in exchange for cryptographic services to the State Department), he hung out a shingle as a psychonumeranalyst. Hard as it may be to believe, he struggled to build a solid customer base. So he became an entertainer, performing a mind-reading act at nightclubs. Along the way, he established a longtime professional relationship with Martin Gardner, a columnist for *Scientific American,* who became Dr. Matrix's Boswell.

Starting in 1960, he'd share with Gardner material that Gardner would incorporate into his columns—incredibly elaborate number puzzles that were both amazing and absolutely not for everybody. Things like hexaflexagons, polyominoes, tangrams, and fractals. But he would also include observations that more casual readers could appreciate. For example, he was credited as the first to point out a darkly fascinating detail in Arthur C. Clarke's novel (and eventually Stanley Kubrick's film) *2001: A Space Odyssey.* If you shifted each letter of the name of the villainous supercomputer HAL forward one letter, it became IBM—the world leader in computer manufacturing. Clarke denied it was on purpose, but Dr. Matrix shrugged it off, insisting even if it wasn't a conscious choice, it wasn't entirely random. Because, according to Dr. Matrix, no numerical or letter patterns are truly random.

"It is naive to suppose that there is such a thing as a randomly arranged group of symbols," he told Gardner in one of their early conversations. "Random means without order or pattern. The term is obviously self-contradictory. You can no more find a patternless arrangement of digits or letters than you can find a cloud without a shape or a culture without folkways."

After providing Gardner with material for numerous columns and embarking on various globetrotting exploits over the next two decades, Dr. Matrix met a fittingly mysterious end in Bucharest in 1980. There he was reportedly shot to death in a duel with a Russian agent while on a secret mission for the CIA. There were rumors that it was all staged—even his funeral—and that Dr. Matrix's fascinating life soldiered on under a different name.

It's an amazing story about a mesmerizing, seemingly supernatural genius.

But none of it was true.

In reality, Dr. Matrix was simply a satirical creation of Gardner, who weaved the character in and out of his *Scientific American* columns with a knowing wink at his readers, who were in on the joke. Most of them, anyway.

"I think for his column," says Gardner's son Jim, himself a Ph.D. and career college professor, "he figured out he could create this character and then he could play around with introducing these interesting numerology things without having it attributed to him. So he did it more in a recreational way as a parody."

Martin Gardner was the real genius, a lifelong admirer of puzzles, magic, and philosophy. He began his "Mathematical Games" column in *Scientific American* in 1956, and it would run for the next 25 years, eventually becoming a library of more than 300 articles. He'd spend 25 days each month working on his column, in which he regularly demonstrated he was one of the most influential and important mathematicians of all time. Through his work, he inspired countless young people to step into the fascinating and often mesmerizing world of mathematics. His admirers included tangential virtuosos like Isaac Asimov, M.C. Escher, and Carl Sagan. Another was Salvador Dalí, who very much wanted to meet Gardner so he could be put in touch with Dr. Matrix. Gardner had to very gently let him in on the hoax.

Gardner himself was fascinated by Lewis Carroll's *Alice in Wonderland* and L. Frank Baum's Oz books, publishing numerous articles and books that explored both fictional worlds and what they represented. But it's important to point out, while Gardner had fun with this type of work, he was a vehement warrior against pseudoscience—things like astrology, pyramid power, homeopathy, and scientology. He spent much of his career debunking these tentacles of fringe science. He was all for having fun, but never at the expense of abandoning rational thought or scientific analysis. Nor did he see his puzzles as simple games. The two primary tenants he believed in were that puzzles, games, and magic were an effective way to get people (young people, in particular) interested in something, and that this interest would lead to further discovery in a field that might otherwise have gone unexplored.

When he died in 2010 at the age of 95, Gardner was rightfully celebrated as an intellectual giant, arguably the most influential mathematician of the twentieth century—even though he never took an advanced mathematics course beyond high school. Through his more than 70 books and countless articles spanning six decades, he entertained, he educated, and most importantly, he showed us a new way to think. And while there are almost certainly more meaningful topics on his resume, the one that may be his most memorable is what brings us to Dr. Matrix.

As Gardner would later explain, one week after John Kennedy was assassinated (and just after Dr. Matrix was released from prison for his counterfeit bills sentence), Gardner received a letter from his enigmatic colleague.

"The two most dramatic and tragic deaths in American political history," the letter began, "were the deaths of Abraham Lincoln and John Fitzgerald Kennedy. There are so many astonishing numerological parallels involving these two events of infamy that I am impelled to record them for you. Please use the following analysis as you wish, but with discretion."

The letter went on to list the coincidences between JFK's assassination and Abraham Lincoln's that we would become familiar with. It was essentially the same list that would eventually be printed on artificially aged paper and hung in poster display racks in museum gift shops across the country.

Martin Gardner didn't publish the list in his column or officially release it to the press, but did circulate it among friends and colleagues. By the following spring, portions of Dr. Matrix's letter were being passed around offices in New York and Washington. After a portion of the list was printed in the GOP Congressional Committee newsletter, in August, both *Time* and *Newsweek* published articles ticking off the coincidences, and we were on our way to their becoming a part of the American lexicon.

Two years later, country singer Buddy Starcher released a spoken-word recording titled "History Repeats Itself" in which he essentially read off Dr. Matrix's list verbatim over the "Battle Hymn of the Republic." Simple as it was, the allure of the subject matter was enough to propel the song to No. 39 on the Billboard Hot 100 chart and No. 2 on the country chart. Cab Calloway would cover it shortly after, and that version also cracked the Hot 100. Unable to cram all of the coincidences into a two-minute 45 record, Starcher went back to the well for a sequel to cram in a few more that weren't included in Dr. Matrix's original list. Some were interesting, albeit not completely accurate, like Lincoln's assassin shot him with a pistol and was later killed with a rifle (actually it was a Colt revolver), while Kennedy's used a rifle, then was killed by a pistol. Starcher also tried to play the same-number-of-letters game with the names of each assassin's assassin, but misidentified Booth's killer. Whoopsies.

Starcher's missteps weren't the only liberties taken with the original list. By the time his recording was in heavy rotation on the radio, a few important changes and deletions had been made. Dr. Matrix included the observation, often cited but not included in the primary spotlight, that Lincoln was killed in Ford's Theatre, while Kennedy was killed in a Lincoln convertible made by the Ford Motor Company. While not fitting into the general "this, then that" structure of the list, that small bouquet of details may be as powerful as anything else in it.

More notably, as Dr. Matrix's letter made the rounds, the personal-secretary coincidence was altered. The original notation pointed out that as the counterbalance to Evelyn Lincoln as Kennedy's secretary, Lincoln's secretary was named "John"—either John Nicolay or John Hay, which are both historically correct—rather than "Kennedy," which is not. And Dr. Matrix's original list mentioned nothing about either secretary providing a cryptic warning to his or her employer. There was a similar scenario with the tweaking of Booth's final destination. Dr. Matrix noted it correctly as a "barn," but it was eventually changed to "warehouse" to mirror Lee Harvey Oswald's choice of location. A similar change was made to the description of the assassins. Dr. Matrix used the phrase "Southerners who held extremist views," which is more on point than the "held unpopular ideas" phrase we eventually wound up with. Nor did Dr. Matrix include the out-of-left-field-and-ultimately-incorrect note about both succeeding vice presidents being opposed for election by men whose names began with G.

In addition to the primary list of coincidences, Dr. Matrix went on to describe quite a few more—some much more complex and, in some ways, more substantial.

Along the same lines as the similarities in the numbers of letters in the various names, Dr. Matrix pointed out how the number six provided a common thread through the JFK assassination:

- If you add the digits of 11/22 together, you get the number six. Friday, the day of the week Kennedy was shot (and also the sixth day of a full week) has six letters.
- Oswald's last name also contained six letters, and he fired the fatal shots from the sixth floor of the Texas School Book Depository.
- If you take "FBI"—which even before the assassination, had been investigating Lee Harvey Oswald after he'd defected to the Soviet Union—and shift each letter six letters ahead, you get "LHO." Oswald's initials.
- And another way of looking at that triple letter shift is to see it as 666—the number of the beast according to the Book of Revelations.

Not that you could really blame the FBI for not picking up on that little cocktail of coincidences. But Dr. Matrix wasn't done. In a bit of Monday-morning quarterbacking that would plague almost all discussions of the Kennedy assassination for years to come, Dr. Matrix pointed out in his letter that "both the Federal Bureau of Investigation and the Secret Service, had they been skilled in the prophetic aspects of numerology, would have been more alert on the fatal day."

To really understand the next observation, it helps to pull out a one-dollar bill. Two weeks before the assassination, Dr. Matrix explained, the Treasury Department released a new series of one-dollar bills. In the circular Federal Reserve seal to the left of George Washington's portrait was a letter K (which, if you want, could stand for Kennedy, but that's immaterial to Dr. Matrix's point).

Then as now, each letter that appears in that circle represents the city and Federal Reserve district in which that bill was produced. And K was assigned to Dallas, Texas, which appears in curved type just beneath the letter.

Creepy, yes. But Dr. Matrix wasn't done.

K is the eleventh letter of the alphabet. "Dallas, Texas" has eleven letters in it, as does "John Kennedy." If you double 11, you get 22, which together form the date of the assassination. Forming an invisible rectangle around Washington's portrait on this new series of bills were four instances of the number eleven—which is Dallas's Federal Reserve district number.

And the serial numbers on each bill in this new series began with a K, again reflecting Dallas's district-letter code. But the number then also ended with the letter "A"—as in "Kennedy Assassination."

Altogether, it was, especially for the time, a lot to unpack.

It's unclear whether Gardner is responsible for discovering each and every entry on the original list. "I suspect he created some under the guise of Dr. Matrix," says Jim Gardner, "but I also suspect he was in the loop for hearing different coincidences through his magic and skeptic connections. He had a network of friends and colleagues who were quick to share things like these interesting coincidences."

But for as much of an impact as the list had and as much as he believed that every pattern had a secret meaning, Martin Gardner himself wasn't quite sure what to draw from all of it. "There are dozens of monumental questions about which I have to say 'I don't know,'" he once said in an interview. "I don't know whether there is intelligent life elsewhere in the universe, or whether life is so improbable that we are truly alone in the cosmos. I don't know whether there is just one universe, or a multiverse in which an infinite number of universes explode into existence, live and die, each with its own set of laws and physical constants. I don't know if quantum mechanics will someday give way to a deeper theory. I don't know whether there is a finite set of basic laws of physics or whether there are infinite depths of structure like an infinite set of Chinese boxes."

Chinese boxes is a fitting analogy. For once Dr. Matrix lifted the lid on this particular box of coincidences, others found countless more inside.

Most focus on similarities—some true, some not quite—between the assassinated presidents themselves. They both had contracted scarlet fever earlier in their lives. The women they married were both 24 at the time of their weddings and spoke fluent French. Before taking office, each man had a sister who died. They were initially elected to Congress exactly 100 years apart. Both were related to a long-term mayor of Boston (Lincoln's cousin and Kennedy's grandfather). Their vice presidents both suffered from ureteral stones. Lincoln had sons named Edward and Robert, Kennedy had brothers by the same name. Lincoln's son Robert married a woman named Mary Eunice, Kennedy had a sister named Eunice Mary. Both men's youngest surviving sons died on July 16 (Tad Lincoln in 1871 of lung disease, John Kennedy, Jr., in a plane crash in 1999).

Others begin to wheeze a bit. They both served in the military, liked sitting in rocking chairs, and appeared to have a lazy right eye. They both appear on coins. They both liked Shakespeare. They both vocalized an acceptance about the reality of the relative ease it would take to shoot a president. Lee Harvey Oswald was named for General Robert E. Lee, who was the military leader of Booth's cause. The most memorable recording of Kennedy's assassination was filmed by a man named *Abraham* Zapruder. Along Booth's escape route, a man named Oswald helped Booth. Oswald was assisted in getting his job at the Texas School Book Depository by a woman named Paine—the same last name as one of Booth's co-conspirators. Both of their wives oversaw an expensive redecoration of the White House after taking office. Both men were wearing Brooks Brothers suits when shot. Eventually both assassinations were rumored to have been orchestrated from within the government.

Still others strain comparative logic to the point of combustion. Things like Lincoln's father was a bartender, while Kennedy's father was a bootlegger. Or that both of their succeeding vice presidents had fathers who were janitors. Stranger still are side-by-side comparisons of photographs of not only Kennedy and Lincoln, but their relatives, vice presidents, favorite poets, advisors, and cabinet members, pointing out physical similarities.

Dr. John Lattimer enthusiastically ticks off dozens of these similarities at the end of his incredibly detailed book comparing the medical and ballistic details of the assassinations. But he also offers a warning: "We must be careful, of course, not to attach more than the proper amount of significance to these similarities; we must, in effect, know how to recognize simple coincidence when we see it."

Jim Gardner tends to agree. "It's purely entertainment," he says. "It's simply if you step back and look at all these numerous potential relationships, you can find something. All it takes is one person to think that something is far more relevant than it really should be, and off they go. It's in our nature to find some sort of order to it that may not be there."

Which, ironically, is often what seems to drive conspiracy theorists, particularly for JFK's assassination. There's a primal need to find a more elaborate, meaningful explanation other than a twerp firing shots at a president because he's pissed at the world. For some, it's actually scarier to believe the randomness of that reality than one in which Kennedy was killed by a vast, Shakespearean plot orchestrated by ghoulishly powerful people.

Curmudgeonly former prosecutor-turned-author Vincent Bugliosi points this out repeatedly in his 1,612-page tome *Reclaiming History*, in which he painstakingly sets out to refute every angle of conspiratorial theory about the JFK assassination. But while he admits that the desire to bring order to chaos is what drives the conspiracy buffs, he passes up the opportunity to dismiss the patterns between the Lincoln and Kennedy assassinations along the same lines. Near the end of his book, he stops in his tracks to list the similarities—essentially as if he were interrupting his broadcast for breaking news. Admitting they don't necessarily have a place in an academic investigation of either assassination, he states that "the coincidences between Lincoln's and Kennedy's lives and deaths are so incredible that one can't help but shake one's head in wonderment and fascination."

Indeed. It's a pinch of historical cognitive dissonance: we know there isn't anything that truly connects these two events, but we tend to believe it anyway. Or, on some level, *want* to believe it. We look up at the night sky and see patterns and shapes among the stars that aren't really there—then point them out to our children and name film production companies after them.

For all the similarities between the two assassinations, there's also evidence (using that word as liberally as possible, of course) to suggest that whatever connects them might not be isolated to just these two events. Not so much evidence, perhaps, but rather an independent anecdote. And maybe not so much an anecdote as something more along the lines of a folk tale. Something that, while maybe a topic of discussion in mythology or theology, doesn't generally come up in the study of American history.

A curse.

Black magic consummated in the spoken word and thrust outward to stretch across two centuries like a dark, vindictive cloud.

3

The Curse of Tippecanoe

If any of the following is to be believed, it all began with a dream. Or, if you're going to go all in, a vision.

Deep within the dark winter months of 1805, a Native American of no real consequence toppled over unconscious. Which wasn't all that unusual. He'd been falling over, both literally and figuratively, his entire life. He wasn't much of a warrior or leader—for instance, he'd accidentally shot out his own eye with a bow and arrow and would wear a patch for the rest of his life. And, unfortunately, as with many of his native brothers during this tragic century, he often sank deep into the hazy fog of firewater. Even in dramatically simpler times, his life was a mess.

So when he passed out in a drunken stupor that winter day, no one could have predicted how it would affect Indian history. Family members and friends discovered him lying on the ground and, depending on which interpretation of the story is being told, either thought that he'd just lost consciousness again or, in the more dramatic version, that he had, in fact, died. In the extended-cut version of this story, his body was actually prepared for burial. Either way, he suddenly sat up and started talking to anyone who would listen about the chilling vision that had come to him, either as an inebriated hallucination or in an ethereal corridor of the afterlife.

He saw himself coming to a fork in a trail, he explained. To the left, where he saw many of his people going, stood three houses. Like himself, most of the Indians he saw traveling along the left side of the path were failures and drunkards. When they reached the third and final house along the path, they were taken inside and forced to drink molten lead. He could hear the screams of pain and anguish echoing from inside the house, where his people were being systematically—yet voluntarily—destroyed.

Along the right side of the path, all was beautiful and idyllic. The lilt of sweet-smelling flowers filled the air and settled over a vast, inviting land that promised fertile ground for planting and ample fields and rivers for hunting and fishing.

He interpreted the vision as not just a metaphor for himself and his life choices, but for all Native Americans. He began to explain what he'd seen to those around him, trembling and weeping under the weight of his emotional awakening. The Great Spirit, he explained, had showed him this vision because of the incorrect path he was taking. If he could reform, other Indians would follow suit. He was convinced he'd been instructed by the Great Spirit to warn all Native Americans of what he'd seen and lead them along the correct path.

He immediately course-corrected his personal journey, giving up alcohol and, for the first time, adopting a clear purpose and direction. He continued to speak to those in his tribe, and as word of his vision and his message spread across the region, others came to hear him.

Previous to this, his name has been Tenskwatawa. But henceforth, he would be known as the Prophet.

Over the next few years, as his celebrity status and followers grew, he honed his message. He encouraged Native Americans to completely disavow white culture and any of its byproducts: alcohol namely, but also their food, clothes, weapons, and tools. Indians should return to their core principles, particularly in this time of seeing their vast continent gradually being swarmed with white settlers.

More controversial, or perhaps innovative, was the Prophet's belief that Native Americans should reject their tribal distinctions and form a single nation. While whites could bamboozle and overwhelm individual tribes one at a time, they couldn't conquer a continent of people connected by a single, unshakable purpose.

As with this story, what happened over the rest of the Prophet's life is open to interpretation and debate. At the heart of these differences is his relationship with his—for modern audiences at least—more famous brother, Tecumseh.

In some ways, Tecumseh is the most well-known Native American, if for no other reason than his being the subject of the life-size wooden statue just beside the entrance to the bar on the hit TV comedy *Cheers*. But long before his long-running sitcom cameo, Tecumseh encapsulated the entire noble, heroic, and tragic experience of the Indian-American conflict. A warrior and leader in the Shawnee tribe, Tecumseh is

Tenskwatawa, known as the Prophet, was a mysterious figure who became part of a legend in which he supposedly cursed seven U.S. presidents to tragic deaths (Smithsonian American Art Museum, Gift of Mrs. Joseph Harrison, Jr.).

remembered as a martyr to the defeated cause of a nation of Indians who spent their lives fighting to preserve what was rightly theirs. First through negotiation, and then in war.

It was Tecumseh who ultimately went down in history as the one with the vision of bringing all the Indians of North America together into one united nation. Whether he took up the cause originally established by his brother the Prophet or the other way around, the most commonly accepted version of what played out is what ultimately leads us to the fable of the curse that connects the assassinations of Lincoln and Kennedy.

Tecumseh spent years building an Indian confederacy, carefully recruiting tribes from all across the uncharted wilderness of North America and uniting them against the whites. His dream was to garner enough strength and numbers to stop the United States' rapid expansion west and force the American government to recognize and respect this new Indian nation. Native Americans would ultimately have geographic and political boundaries clearly outlined across the continent just like all other countries—in essence, sharing North America with the U.S. alongside Canada and Mexico.

Of course, a story like this needs a villain, and playing that role—at least subjectively—was William Henry Harrison. If the name sounds familiar at all, it's likely due to his rather insubstantial legacy as the U.S. president with the shortest term in office (which will become a big factor in this story). This version of Harrison is a young, ambitious military leader who fought against the Indians throughout the Midwest in the late eighteenth century. His resume included the Battle of Fallen Timbers in 1792, where he and Tecumseh, fighting among the Shawnee warriors in the battle, initially crossed paths.

Harrison transitioned into politics. He was appointed governor of the Indiana territory in 1800, a role in which he oversaw a region much larger than what the state of Indiana would become. The primary purposes of his tenure were, for all intentions, contradictory: to calm the rising tensions between Indians and white settlers in the region, while also acquiring as much land for white settlement as possible. He leaned toward the latter, and was embraced and revered by the white settlers for it—laying the initial foundation for his eventual path to the White House.

Obviously, Harrison saw Tecumseh and the Prophet as threats to both of his objectives, albeit for different reasons. Tecumseh was, Harrison wrote, "one of those uncommon geniuses which spring up occasionally to produce revolutions and overturn the established order of things." The Prophet, on the other hand, Harrison saw as a fraud. Amazed by the dedication of the Prophet's followers, Harrison tried to tell them that the Prophet was nothing of the kind. He suggested in a letter to them that they demand the Prophet prove he was truly deserving of the name. "Ask him to curse the sun to stand still," he even suggested. Had he chosen his words more carefully or at least not provided such a specific suggestion, things might have unfolded differently. Instead, in June of 1806, the Prophet gave a rousing speech in which he demanded that the sun go dark. And shortly after, there was a solar eclipse.

Most agree that the Prophet somehow knew that the eclipse was coming. He then used the knowledge—and Harrison's regrettably specific challenge—to his advantage, rather than just getting amazingly lucky or, of course, actually causing the sun to go dark. However it went down, that round went to the Prophet, whose reputation and power increased dramatically.

As his community grew around him, the Prophet formed his own settlement in 1808 and not-so-humbly named it Prophetstown. Located near what is now West Lafayette, Indiana, it became the epicenter of the cause he and Tecumseh were leading, and the settlement grew over the next several years as more and more Indians joined their ranks.

By 1811, Prophetstown had grown to the point that white settlers in the region demanded something be done about it. Harrison led a contingent of about 1000 soldiers to the area. On November 6, the contingent stopped just outside Prophetstown at a small outpost called Tippecanoe. What exactly Harrison intended is not entirely clear. He had orders from Washington to avoid conflict if at all possible, and he'd intended the primary purpose of his jaunt to be negotiation. True enough, he'd scheduled a council for the following day. But the 1000 soldiers he'd brought along suggested he was fully prepared for something else—if not to attack, then perhaps to lure the Indians into a battle they couldn't win.

The Prophet took the bait. With the more battle-savvy Tecumseh away, the Prophet ignored his brother's advice to avoid any conflict with Harrison until he returned. Even though he was badly outnumbered, the Prophet ordered an attack, reportedly assuring his followers that they couldn't be defeated. He covered his warriors with sacred clay and told them that the white soldiers' bullets would turn to mud and bounce off of them.

Before dawn on November 7, the Prophet's Indians attacked

Harrison's camp. Initially caught off guard, the soldiers suffered many casualties in the confused darkness. But as the sun began to rise, Harrison launched a counter attack, and the battle turned. The Indians were quickly defeated and retreated back to Prophetstown, where a subdued and embarrassed Prophet now ordered that they evacuate their village before the troops invaded.

When Harrison's troops arrived at Prophetstown, they discovered it completely abandoned. After taking what supplies they found, Harrison ordered his troops to burn the village to the ground. From their encampment a few miles away, the defeated Indians could see the plumes of smoke on the horizon and knew what was happening. When they returned to the smoldering ashes of Prophetstown, they were shocked by what they saw. The triumphant soldiers hadn't just destroyed their homes and food supply for the winter—they'd also dug up Indian graves and desecrated the bodies. This was a violation that could not be forgiven nor forgotten. And the Prophet would remember.

Despite the pillaging and victorious destruction, the Battle of Tippecanoe as it came to be known was not exactly a triumph for the American side. They'd suffered significant casualties—nearly 200 troops either killed or injured. But with Harrison looking to enhance his career and Washington desperate for good news from the quagmire of the wilderness, it would be celebrated as a rousing success. For the dream of uniting Native Americans into one single nation, it would go down in history as a devastating setback. The Prophet's magical reputation was obviously tainted, and many of his followers abandoned him. It now also became much harder to convince other tribes to believe in the cause.

When Tecumseh returned, he was furious with his brother. "In one day," he is to have said, "you have destroyed what I have taken over ten summers to build and which now can never be rebuilt. In one day you have destroyed the hopes of all Indians. You are a liar, a cheat, a fool filled with the lust of power.... You are no longer my brother. You are no longer a Shawnee, nor even an Indian. You are dishonored as no man has ever before been dishonored." Tecumseh

The Battle of Tippecanoe was a devastating turning point in the quest to form an Indian nation, in which the Prophet's warriors were routed by federal troops (led by William Henry Harrison portrayed at far left, on horseback) in November 1811 (Library of Congress).

grabbed him by the hair and violently shook his head. He then held a knife to his throat and threatened to kill him before deciding that was too honorable a fate for this disgraced heretic who had been his brother.

Tecumseh would continue to fight for Indian land and justice, eventually dying at the Battle of Thames in 1813 during the War of 1812. Fighting against—you guessed it—the villain of this tale, William Henry Harrison. And here's where it all comes full circle. Even though Harrison didn't kill Tecumseh personally (no one knows for sure who actually did), the fact that Harrison ultimately led the force that was responsible for his death, on top of all his other injustices against Native Americans over the years, was enough to rile the anger of the Prophet.

Disgraced from the debacle at Prophetstown, the Prophet ventured further west, eventually settling in what is now Missouri, where he'd spend the rest of his days. Perhaps stewing in bitterness, he watched as Harrison's career evolved: elected to Congress and then the U.S. Senate. When Harrison became a realistic candidate for the presidency in 1836, the Prophet, from his death bed, reportedly spoke words that, if to be believed, would alter the course of American history.

"Harrison will not win this year to be the Great Chief," the Prophet is to have said. "But he may win next year. If he does ... he will not finish his term. He will die in his office. You think I have lost my powers. I who caused the sun to darken and the Red Man to give up firewater.... I tell you Harrison will die. And after him every Great Chief chosen every 20 years thereafter will die. And when each one dies, let everyone remember the death of our people."

Sometime not long after allegedly speaking those words, the Prophet died.

Harrison did not get elected in 1836, just as the Prophet predicted, but he was elected in 1840 (presumably the "next year" the Prophet referred to). Alongside his running mate John Tyler, Harrison built a strong following on the strength of a formidable grass roots campaign that primarily focused on Harrison's background as a war hero. The most memorable aspect of that election was Harrison's campaign phrase "Tippecanoe and Tyler Too"—stapling his victory over the Prophet to his political identity as a nickname.

At age 67, Harrison was the oldest man ever elected president at the time. After giving a lengthy inaugural address in rainy, cold weather with no coat, he caught a bad cold that turned to pneumonia and died one month into his term—the shortest of any president in history. More modern scientific research suggests that the real cause of Harrison's death may not have been a long speech in bad weather as has long been accepted, but rather a tainted water supply near the White House. Whether caused by hubris in bad weather or an inadequate drainage system, the end result is the same: one month after becoming president, Harrison was dead.

An amazing coincidence or a curse? Or perhaps neither.

Adding fuel to the fire of the curse theory, over the next 120

An adversary to both Tecumseh and the Prophet, William Henry Harrison later became the first president to die in office—thus beginning the so-called "Curse of Tippecanoe" (Library of Congress).

years, each president elected in a year ending in a zero died in office—just as the Prophet supposedly predicted.

There was Lincoln, of course, in 1860, followed by the two members of our assassinated presidents control group: James Garfield, elected in 1880, and William McKinley, re-elected in 1900. Warren

Harding came along in 1920 and died abruptly of heart failure three years later, and then we had Franklin Roosevelt's second re-election in 1940, five years before his death following his third re-election. The bookend was John Kennedy, elected in 1960 and the seventh president in the series to die in office.

It became known as the Presidential Curse or Tecumseh's Curse, even though Tecumseh had nothing to do with it. Today it's more widely known as the Curse of Tippecanoe—turning Harrison's catchy and electable nickname back around as the cause of all this dark magic.

Taken at face value, it's a chilling little tale. And if you believe at all in this type of thing, there's just enough circumstantial evidence there for you to buy into it. But to be fair, there are problems with the story, primarily large swaths of details that are dramatically open to interpretation.

First and foremost, the Prophet's curse seems (a) incredibly random and (b) bizarrely slow-acting. To put the whammy on William Henry Harrison out of vengeance is, in a relative sense at least, understandable. But why wait to activate the curse until he became president? And why then carry it through to anyone else who just happened to hold the same job (which, by the way, Harrison did not hold at the time of the cursing but seemed to be the principal ingredient)? And why not *all* of the presidents that came after him instead of just those elected in years that end in zero? Was a president elected in one of those years more deserving of death than the guy elected four years earlier? Admittedly, curses may not be put together like Ikea furniture, but even if you believe in this story, it would be hard to explain or justify the Prophet's scattershot recipe for disaster.

Likewise, why wait nearly three decades to enact sanctimonious revenge? If the trigger for the curse was Harrison ordering the desecration of the Indian burial ground at Prophetstown (often cited as the Prophet's ultimate motivation and which, by its nature, does sound like something that would open yourself up to some seriously dark juju), 25 years would pass between that incident and the Prophet laying down the hammer. And even then, the curse itself would not actually kick in for another five years after that. Holding a grudge is one thing, but cursing someone to a disgraceful death sure feels like something you'd do in the heat of the moment, doesn't it? Not a generation later as if it were an afterthought line item in an appropriations bill.

Perhaps more telling, there's no historical chain of evidence for this story. There's no record of anyone mentioning the Prophet or a curse following Harrison's death in 1841, or for that matter, the 20-year aspect of the curse following the assassinations of Lincoln, Garfield, or McKinley. The first mention of any connection came in 1931 in a *Ripley's Believe It or Not* column. Even then, the deaths (at this point five of them following Harding's passing) were simply presented as an interesting coincidence with no point of origin. The word "curse" was never bandied about until syndicated cartoonist John Hix used it in a column in 1940. A man wrote a letter pointing out this "historical curiosity" to then–Senator John Kennedy in 1959 as he mulled over a presidential run. Kennedy actually wrote the man back, replying that "the future will necessarily answer" his fate, should he have "the privilege of occupying the White House." The following year, as Kennedy marched toward the 1960 election, the torch was picked up by another journalist, Ed Koterba, in an article that fall. But none of these instances mentioned Tippecanoe, Tecumseh, or the Prophet.

The first time these threads were all drawn together wasn't until 1980. As we again led up to the apex of the apparent 20-year cycle, celebrity gossip columnist Lloyd Shearer put it all together in *Parade* magazine. It was at this point that the curse truly entered the American headspace and the sudden origin story became generally accepted as fact.

Even the candidates themselves became aware of it. As Jimmy Carter was running for re-election that fall, a reporter asked him if he was concerned about the apparent 20-year cycle at a campaign event in Dayton, Ohio. "I've seen those predictions.... I'm not afraid," Carter replied. "If I knew it was going to happen, I would go ahead and be president and do the best I could until the last day I could." In a chilling twist, in the crowd hearing those words was would-be presidential assassin John Hinckley. He had begun stalking the president along the campaign trail with the intention of shooting him to prove himself worthy to actress Jodie Foster. Hinckley would eventually change his choice of target to Ronald Reagan after the election and succeed in shooting (and very nearly killing) the new president in March 1981. Though unarmed that afternoon in Dayton, he'd managed to come within six feet of Carter, who'd just boldly stated that he wasn't afraid of the specter of assassination.

Nancy Reagan also didn't pay much attention to the topic in 1980 as her husband was running for president. But after he was shot and nearly killed two months into his term, she saw it in a different light. "Now that my own husband was president and an attempt had been made on his life," she wrote in her memoir, "the historical pattern became terrifying to me.... Was the shooting in March 1981 merely an omen, an early warning that something even worse might lie ahead?"

More as a superstitious comfort than a core belief, Nancy Reagan began to consult with a San Francisco astrologer named Joan Quigley about the president's schedule. Quigley never advised on political matters, the First Lady was quick to point out, but merely on what were favorable and unfavorable days (since Mrs. Reagan had learned after the fact that March 30, 1981, had been a "dangerous" day for her husband). "While I was never certain that Joan's astrological advice was helping to protect Ronnie," she admitted, "the fact is that nothing like March 30 ever happened again."

Indeed it did not. And there's a theory that this is what enabled Reagan to snap the presidential curse, as he survived both of his terms—the first president elected in a year ending in zero to do so since James Monroe. George W. Bush did the same after being elected in 2000. Perhaps astrology was the antidote to the curse that had plagued seven presidents over the course of 120 years.

Or maybe there is no reason why it came to an end. Perhaps curses do have an expiration date. There's also the possibility there never was one in the first place.

Even if there is no clear origin story or resolution, the 20-year presidential death cycle is a creepy little coincidence, and yet another thread tying the Lincoln and Kennedy assassinations together.

Not unlike the little-known story about how John Kennedy saved Abraham Lincoln's life.

4.

That Time John Kennedy Saved Abraham Lincoln

Okay, fine, not *that* John Kennedy.

As evidenced earlier, there's fun to be had with other gentlemen in history that share that relatively common name (but are still connected to Lincoln in relatively uncommon ways). And while the statistically pedestrian nature of the name may be enough for the naysayers to poo-poo this entire story (just as they could have with the John Kennedy-as-Lincoln's-running-mate connection), there's enough there to render this a tale of some note.

But before we get to the story of how Kennedy saved Lincoln, it's best to set the stage by pointing out that Abraham Lincoln could very easily have been assassinated long before he actually was.

Let's work backward from John Wilkes Booth's murder of the president in April 1865. While ultimately successful, strategically speaking, it wasn't the smartest time to pull it off. After all, the war was over. Robert E. Lee's Army of Northern Virginia had surrendered just days before, and after a week of celebration and relief in Washington, focus was beginning to turn toward reconciliation. Lincoln had already begun to outline his vision for reconstruction, and it was not a vengeful one.

This sentiment was reflected in what would be the final speech he ever gave. On Tuesday evening, April 11, just three nights before he would be shot, Lincoln gave an impromptu address from a White House balcony to a crowd primarily made up of revelers, still basking in the glow of victory. And, in what proved to be a fateful comment, he proposed the idea of giving Blacks the right to vote in this reconciled nation.

Down below in the crowd looking up at Lincoln from the White House lawn stood John Wilkes Booth. When he heard Lincoln's words, his blood boiled. "That means (n-word) citizenship," Booth commented to a friend standing beside him. "Now, by God, I'll put him through. That is the last speech he will ever make."

Indeed it was, because Booth's hatred and inherent racism drove him to the act of murder. But while he may have harbored some notion of reviving the Confederate cause by murdering Lincoln (along with, potentially at least, Vice President Andrew Johnson and Secretary of State William Seward, as was his plan), it was, even at the time, pure nonsense. In fact, rather than giving the Confederacy a second life, Booth actually made things far worse for his beloved South. The vengeance Lincoln was going to resist became a huge part of the plan for reconstruction in the South after the president's death—in large part because of the residual anger for what Booth had done and why.

If Booth truly wanted to achieve anarchic confusion or political instability, Lincoln would have needed to be removed from office in the midst of war. Which was, to be fair, Booth's original plan. Booth's initial pathway into historical infamy was a clown-shoes kidnapping scheme in which he and the same group of conspirators he would roll with on April 14 would spirit Lincoln away and exchange him for Confederate POWs. Booth even initially suggested that, like his eventual assassination plan, the kidnapping should take place in Ford's Theatre. He suggested his team could lower Lincoln down to the stage from the presidential box as a theatre full of spectators watched, and then spirit him away. Booth had even reserved the presidential box for himself and his friends to see a performance on March 15, 1865, and scout out the setting for his proposed kidnapping caper. It's almost hard to believe that his fellow conspirators voted down the idea at a late dinner after the show.

A more plausible possibility opened up two days later when Booth discovered Lincoln would be attending a play for wounded Union soldiers at Campbell Hospital just outside of Washington. Booth hurriedly assembled his team with the plan of snatching Lincoln on a small, isolated road on the way to the hospital. But when the president's plans changed at the last moment (ironically, to give a speech at the hotel at which Booth was staying), the team thought its plan had been discovered and scattered. The following evening, Booth gave what would be the final performance of his acting career in *The Apostate* at Ford's Theatre. Or, depending on how you look at it, his final performance actually happened 27 nights later on the same stage after leaping from the presidential box.

While Booth's slapdash kidnapping plots died on the vine, another apparent attempt on Lincoln's life came perilously close to succeeding nine months before Ford's Theatre. On an August night in 1864, Lincoln was riding a horse to the cabin he and his family often visited near the Old Soldiers' Home just a few miles outside of Washington. Along the path, a sniper fired a shot from the forest that was close enough to knock Lincoln's hat off. When the hat was found later, there was a bullet hole in the side, just inches from where Lincoln's head had been. Who fired the shot was never discovered, and the president passed off the incident as a hunting accident—which, in theory, it could have been—and didn't want it shared.

But all of these near misses paled in comparison to the most mysterious and dangerous threat Lincoln faced, when there was a very real possibility of his being murdered even before he became president.

With the nation already teetering on the brink of war in 1860, Lincoln's victory in a polarizing election served as justification for the South to go to the mattresses. Most pro-slavery Southern loyalists hated Lincoln and everything he stood for even before he became president. In the three months between the election and his March 4 inauguration—as seven Southern states seceded from the Union—he received numerous pieces of hate mail and death threats at his home in Springfield, Illinois. As the time drew near for him to begin his long journey to the nation's capital to begin his term, a much more specific and viable threat emerged.

Whispers swirled that a Southern group was planning to blow up the railroad tracks just north of Baltimore as Lincoln made his final approach into Washington. Samuel Morse Felton, president of the Philadelphia, Wilmington, and Baltimore Railroad, got wind of the plot and notified Allan Pinkerton, head of the well-known Pinkerton National Detective Agency. Pinkerton immediately traveled to Baltimore along with a handful of his best agents and went undercover to learn what he could, just as Lincoln was about to begin his 13-stop journey from Illinois to Washington. They quickly discovered this was more than just a threat against the railroad to prevent the inauguration—it was a plot to assassinate Abraham Lincoln during his short stay in Baltimore.

Lincoln's itinerary along his 12-day journey across the country had been made public, including his schedule in each city he stopped. Gradually, Pinkerton pieced together the prospective assassination plan. In the primarily pro-slavery city of Baltimore, an angry crowd would gather around Lincoln as he traveled from one train station to another to board the train to D.C. With the police overmatched and distracted, an assassin would shoot the president-elect and escape into the mob. Pinkerton knew what marginal protection Lincoln would have with him would be unable to prevent such an attack. With Lincoln's arrival in Baltimore just two days away, Pinkerton needed to whip together a plan to stop it and then get in touch with Lincoln along his route and convince him of the danger.

But in what's both a startling and hilarious symbol of American bureaucracy run amok, another official government investigation into the rumors of assassination was taking place by a completely separate group—each totally unbeknownst to the other.

Around the same time that Pinkerton was being summoned to meet with railroad president Felton, John A. Kennedy, the superintendent of the New York Police Department, was called to Washington to have a very similar conversation. Like Felton, friends of Abraham Lincoln in the capital had heard the same rumors and wanted to take whatever action possible to protect the new president. Kennedy had a secret briefing with an official he would later decline to name, and the superintendent was asked for his assistance. Just like Pinkerton, Kennedy traveled to Baltimore along with a pair of undercover detectives to investigate. For the next several weeks, Pinkerton's men and Kennedy's men worked secretly with the same mission—totally unaware of each other and perhaps even crossing paths along the way. Even their channels of communication were tangled: Pinkerton was in direct contact with Lincoln's entourage as it steamed east, while Kennedy sent his information back to Colonel Charles P. Stone in Washington. Once receiving Kennedy's report, Stone got a message to his superior, General Winfield Scott, who told Senator William Seward—who was about to become Lincoln's secretary of state. Seward directed his son Frederick to hop on a train to Philadelphia and deliver this message to Lincoln—just as Pinkerton was boarding another train from Baltimore to do the exact same thing.

Eye-rolling government stereotypes of redundant discombobulation aside, this story has a happy ending. Lincoln was convinced (by whom precisely remains debatable) that the threat was real and his schedule was revised. Rather than arriving in Baltimore at midday on February 23, he was snuck aboard an earlier train out of Philadelphia—a public train whose passengers had no idea that their new president was among them. He arrived in Baltimore at 3:30 a.m., was carefully and quietly transferred to another train, and arrived in Washington just before sunrise. When the would-be Baltimore assassins assembled later that morning to orchestrate their nefarious plot (interestingly, on the same spot where the Baltimore Orioles now play baseball at charming Camden Yards), they had no target to shoot at. They had been bamboozled and checkmated. John Kennedy had saved Abraham Lincoln's life. Or perhaps it was actually Allan Pinkerton who saved Lincoln's life.

In 1867—six years after the averted assassination attempt in Baltimore and two years after the successful one at Ford's Theatre—the *New York Times* published an article that heralded John Kennedy and his men for saving the president's life prior to his inauguration. It didn't mention Pinkerton. The detective, who'd continued his covert work gathering military intelligence for the Union during the war, countered by writing and printing a small pamphlet rebutting Kennedy's take and telling his version of the story for the first time. Pinkerton said that Kennedy, who had been taking credit for saving the president's life, had not played a major role. In fact, Pinkerton said, Kennedy had traveled to Baltimore on the same train as Lincoln but didn't even know that the president-elect was on board.

Kennedy, naturally, felt exactly the opposite. It was, he felt, the message to Lincoln gathered by Kennedy's men and delivered by Frederick Seward that ultimately convinced Lincoln that his life was in danger. And, Kennedy pointed out, throughout the adventure, he had no idea Pinkerton was involved. Which, according to Pinkerton, was by design.

There's evidence to suggest Pinkerton's version is much closer to what really happened. Three days after Lincoln arrived in Washington, Kennedy had written to Pinkerton—not knowing that Pinkerton had been in Baltimore (or on the train) with the president—offering his full cooperation in Washington to continue to protect the president from the threat against his life. Then, two days after that, Kennedy sent a letter to Baltimore police superintendent George P. Kane saying that "there was no foundation in the story" of the assassination threat against Lincoln. A few years later, Kennedy built a reputation as the president's savior on the same foundation of the threat he'd earlier said didn't exist. While Kennedy certainly was involved in investigating the threat, his subsequent actions do reek of shameless self-promotion.

Of course, there's room for more than one hero in this tale. You could argue that Lincoln needed evidence from both groups to be convinced. Conversely, it's possible you could remove either Pinkerton or Kennedy from the story and it would have turned out the same way. Be that as it may, both Allan Pinkerton and John Kennedy deserve credit for parallel-pathing a solution to the assassination plot. It's a complicated, fascinating, and rarely told story that sounds like it could be a movie.

As it turns out, it was.

**

One look at the poster for *The Tall Target* and you think, "This looks like hot garbage."

It's pure pulp silliness. A chisel-chinned Sinatra wannabe stares pensively out at the viewer, framed beside the face of a random woman who's equally afraid about whatever has him feeling pensive. Below them are the silhouettes of a prostrate man atop another on a set of railroad tracks, either attempting to strangle him or performing an overly intense dental procedure. Clearly, with a poster like this, there are several potential trajectories, and a foiled presidential assassination attempt isn't one of them.

As if unable to contain its own excitement, the poster has two equally bizarre taglines. The first, "A Girl Whose Lovely Hands Were Never Meant to Hold a Gun," might as well be an eye exam for as little relevance as it has to the story. The other ejaculates, "You'll never see the target till the very end!" Why that would be a selling point is a fantastic question, but technically, it's correct. Abraham Lincoln, the tall target the title refers to, does not appear in the film until literally the final minute, when he suddenly materializes like Nick Fury, almost as if in a post-credit scene intended to set up the sequel (*Tall Target 2: Ford's Theatre*, perhaps). For in this story, while hovering over each scene, Lincoln is actually little more than a MacGuffin to be sought after and/or protected.

The poster also suggests a very casual relationship with historical accuracy. One look at it and you really don't have any sense that it's a period piece or supposed to be based on a true story. Indeed, in a 2009 look-back at the movie, *America's Civil War* magazine concluded that it was "a classic example of how Hollywood can take a historical incident and sprinkle it with real and imagined characters to create a cinematic public memory that blurs the line between truth and fiction." Considering the film's pedigree, historical accuracy shouldn't be expected. Director Anthony Mann had built his career on westerns and detective stories, while the story and screenplay were credited to George Worthing Yates, who'd made his bones writing serials like *The Lone Ranger* and would later be known for crafting sci-fi schlock like *Them!* and *Earth vs. the Flying Saucers.*

Yet for all its genetic warning flags and creative liberties taken, *The Tall Target* is actually a better movie than it has any right to be. Not that there are many opinions about it, positive or negative. Released in August of 1951, it's now essentially forgotten, inaccessible through any streaming format and available only via DVD from the bowels of Amazon.com like a deep-sea creature that has never seen the light of the sun.

While it wasn't exactly a star-making vehicle, it wound up including a few fun Where's Waldo moments. Grandpa Walton, played by actor Will Geer, is the conductor of the fateful train that propels both the characters and the narrative. A young Barbara Billingsley—June Cleaver herself—has a small role as a mother traveling with her mischievous son who could very well pass for the Beaver. But the most substantial of these "look-who-it-is" roles is played by eventual Emmy winner and Oscar nominee Ruby Dee, who jumps off the screen as the slave Rachel traveling with her "family" back to the South.

The movie's most interesting aspect isn't its fascinating tap dance between adhering to historical accuracy and completely ignoring it. Rather, it's the choice of its central character. For as easy as it would have been to position the more historically well-known Allan Pinkerton as its protagonist, the celluloid version of the rope-a-dope pulled on the Baltimore conspirators chooses John Kennedy as its hero.

Or at least names its hero John Kennedy. Not only does the character in the movie bear no resemblance to the actual police superintendent he's based upon, but he also bears no resemblance to the nineteenth century. *The Tall Target*'s John Kennedy is essentially Sam Spade parachuted into the 1860s, complete with a trench coat and fedora and Bogart-esque dialogue. Which, while a bit out of place in a scene with antebellum ladies dressed like Scarlett O'Hara debating secession, is right in step with the tone of the movie.

This is a film noir murder mystery, the kind of movie that buttered the bread of filmgoers in the 1940s and '50s. It falls right in the comfort zone of director Mann and lead actor Dick Powell, who each built their Hollywood careers in the fictional dark alleys roamed by weathered gumshoes and sultry femme fatales. Shadowy and suspicious, the film is essentially a long night's journey into day that sees an isolated hero risk his career and his life trying to save the president on a train packed with villains out to kill them both.

From the jump, it does take itself seriously. It opens with a prologue crawl that looks and feels like what we'd come to associate with a *Star Wars* movie:

> *Ninety years ago a lonely traveler boarded the night train from New York to Washington, D.C., and when he reached his destination, his passage had become a forgotten chapter in the history of the United States. This motion picture is a dramatization of that disputed journey.*

A disputed dramatization to be sure. We first hear of our hero when a colleague describes him to train conductor Grandpa Walton with a James Bond-ish introduction: "His name's Kennedy. John Kennedy." We then flash to police headquarters, where Sergeant Kennedy—not Superintendent Kennedy—bursts into a smoke-filled room filled with NYPD brass, pleading with them to act upon the Lincoln assassination threat that Kennedy has uncovered. In a strange twist, the person he's trying to convince is the superintendent, who, in reality, was the actual John Kennedy. Perhaps shifting the character's job to sergeant makes the action-adventure tale to follow more believable than saddling Kennedy with a title that suggested he was a bureaucratic bobblehead behind a desk.

Movie Kennedy is laughed out of the room and ordered to stand down. Instead, Kennedy tosses his badge on the desk and quits the force, then heads to the train station en route to Baltimore to try to prevent the assassination by himself. His first step is to try to send an urgent telegram to Philadelphia to warn the president-elect of the threat. Through the lens of our creepy little coincidence, it provides us with a chilling moment: we see the telegram addressed to Abraham Lincoln, from John Kennedy, as if a message from the future to the past.

The movie then shifts comfortably into noir whodunit potboiler. Kennedy becomes tangled in a web of deception and mystery on board the aptly named Night Flyer as it steams through the winter darkness down the eastern seaboard. He learns that his partner has been killed, discovering the body dangling off the caboose, and realizes that the murderer thought he was killing Kennedy. He finds the culprit and they confront one another during a stop at New Brunswick, wrestling on the tracks just as the engine begins to pull out. The murderer is shot and killed by a Union colonel named Jeffers, who then comments to Kennedy, "I don't know anything about a plot against Lincoln's life, but there certainly seems to be one against yours."

Kennedy teams up with Jeffers and reveals what he knows. Two weeks before, Kennedy had been on assignment in Baltimore. He didn't find his suspect, but he uncovered the plot against Lincoln, making friends with the leader of the conspiracy and joining his secret society undercover. We quickly discover the fictional Jeffers is secretly part of the assassination plot, and that the assassin is on the train. The remainder of the film becomes a game of cat and mouse, with Jeffers hunting Kennedy while Kennedy tries to track down the assassin. Little do they (or the audience) know, a mysterious, cloaked passenger that quietly boarded in Philadelphia is actually Abraham Lincoln.

The emotional climax of the film takes place just after Kennedy discovers the assassin—a strapping Southern soldier named Lance, who could be straight out of the Young Colonel Sanders Chronicles. Having received assistance in cracking the case from Ruby Dee's Rachel, Kennedy is held at gunpoint by Lance's sister Ginny, who orders Rachel to go inform her brother figure/owner. Rachel refuses, volleying Ginny's comment about why Rachel never needed to ask for her freedom with "Freedom isn't a thing you should be able to give me, Miss Ginny. Freedom is something I should have been born with." Pretty heady stuff for separate-drinking-fountains 1951 America.

Kennedy is bound and gagged and overhears Jeffers discussing the case with the mastermind behind it—Baltimore barber Cipriano Ferrandini (though pronounced "Ferrandina" for some reason in the movie). An amalgam of Sweeney Todd and Snidely Whiplash, Ferrandini outlines the plot for the audience in a mostly unnecessary exposition dump with almost to-the-letter historical accuracy. The villains discover that Lincoln's Baltimore event has been cancelled, but as the train car pulls out for Washington, Lance the Country Fried Assassin is tipped off that Lincoln is actually on board the same train and begins to search for him. Kennedy escapes and grapples with Lance, tossing him from the train to his death.

With the fictionalized last gasp of the film's version of the assassination plot taken care of, Kennedy is thanked for his service by a Mrs. Gibbons, one of Pinkerton's agents. She's a cinematic (and surprisingly accurate) version of Kate Warne, who had worked for Pinkerton for five years and, as a woman working as an undercover detective in the 1860s, probably deserves her own movie. Earlier in the film, we saw Mrs. Gibbons smuggle a cloaked Lincoln on board the train in Philadelphia—mirroring Warne getting Lincoln on the train under the veil of claiming he was her invalid brother.

The final shot of the film pans past a content and somewhat clueless Pinkerton, who blithely comments that "the journey was without incident," and settles on a resigned Lincoln. Honest Abe sighs, "Did ever any president come to his inauguration so like a thief in the night," as the train glides past the U.S. Capitol Building with its signature dome still only half-built. It's symbolic of America's status of the time, of course, but also of the film's half-accurate depiction of what really happened that February night.

For its over-the-top moments of 1950s fake-punch action, *The Tall Target* does at least acknowledge—though a bit clumsily—that there were two distinct efforts to save Lincoln's life. And it also adheres to what appears to be the accurate detail that Kennedy didn't know that he was on the same train as Lincoln and Pinkerton steaming into Washington. But while Pinkerton does make a cameo at the end, the film posits that the only reason Pinkerton was brought in to protect Lincoln along his journey was because Kennedy had cc'd a copy of his initial report to the War Department. It then had subcontracted Pinkerton—suggesting that Pinkerton hadn't also uncovered and infiltrated the plot on his own. It's this revelation, even more than Kennedy's *Die Hard* adventure on the train, that truly stiff-arms historical accuracy. Evidently, there was only room for one hero if such a complicated story was going to be shoehorned into a 78-minute runtime. But hey, it's Hollywood. Historical accuracy is a big expense.

You also have to wonder if the choice of protagonist would have been different just a few years later. At the time of the film's release, the John Kennedy who would eventually become *the* John Kennedy was wallowing in the House of Representatives in relative anonymity, still nearly nine years away from launching a madcap bid for the presidency. It's fair to wonder, had this movie been made a decade or so later, if Kennedy still would have been chosen as the main character. Perhaps by then, the idea of focusing on a character who would save the president with the same name as *another* president might be a little too much to believe.

Instead, with its sort-of-historically accurate choice of protagonist, the movie underlines a portion of the truth in such a way that it adds another log on the fire of curious coincidences—proclaiming a clear statement on the silver screen for the world to see.

That John Kennedy saved Abraham Lincoln.

5

The X-100 and
the Bloody Rocker

In terms of time, the Lincoln and Kennedy assassinations are separated by 98 years, 7 months, and 8 days.

In terms of geography, Ford's Theatre and Dealey Plaza are separated by 1,330 miles—almost exactly one half the length of the continental United States.

But the actual vessels of these heart-wrenching moments in American history—Lincoln's rocking chair and Kennedy's limousine—in which each man was struck and fell, are separated by a mere 117 steps. Those vast canyons of time, distance, and profound significance can be bridged in roughly a minute, by walking from one section of the Henry Ford Museum to another.

Which is mind-blowing in a variety of ways, as is how these monumentally important artifacts in American history inadvertently and independently wound up in the same place. And that this place would be Dearborn, Michigan, which has absolutely nothing to do with either president or his respective assassination.

Aside from being the home of the Henry Ford Museum, Dearborn—often called "Deadborn" by resident teenagers while staring at their phones—doesn't have much of an identity among most Americans. A suburb of Detroit, Dearborn has gained the distinction in recent years of having the largest Muslim population of any city in the United States. Not at all a recent trend, those numbers have increased gradually since the first wave arrived in the 1880s and has grown ever since by immigrants seeking work or sanctuary from war-torn regions of the world. This newer vision of Dearborn is an interesting parallel to its better-known reputation as the birthplace

of Henry Ford, one of America's great heroes of invention and industry and, unfortunately, also one of America's most notorious anti–
Semites—making Dearborn's claim to fame as America's Muslim
capital darkly ironic.

Following his immense success inventing and then selling the
automobile, Ford became a collector of historical artifacts. He eventually decided to create a showcase for them to be presented to the
public in his old hometown. He originally called it the Edison Insti-
tute of Technology to honor his lifelong hero Thomas Edison, and it
opened in phases: an outdoor village in 1929 followed by an adjacent
indoor museum in 1933. Over time, each section was relabeled as
the much more customer-friendly Greenfield Village and Henry Ford
Museum. Both remain open today as separate yet thematically similar experiences, sort of an industrial/historical version of Walt Disney
World.

Of course, neither experience is specifically focused on assassination, or even presidential history. So to learn that it serves as the
final resting place for perhaps the two most important artifacts in
arguably the two most important single moments in American history is a jarring revelation. And leads to two separate yet equally fascinating stories.

"A lot of people are surprised that they're really not displayed
together," says Matt Anderson, Curator of Transportation at the
Henry Ford Museum. "They're not even a part of the same exhibit
and never have been. We interpret each one in a different way. At the
end of the day, it's just amazing that those two pieces are under the
same roof. But entirely coincidental."

Coincidental indeed. But coincidences are what we're all about
between the covers of this book.

Let's start with the one that does feel genuinely at home in its
surroundings. The 1961 Lincoln Continental limousine in which
John Kennedy was shot fits nicely in a museum named after the man
who basically created the automobile. It's surrounded by a caval-
cade of other cars which all carry some manner of historical import,
though obviously none quite as significant. But more than that, the
car seems to belong here because this is essentially where it was both

born and later reborn in the course of its quietly amazing, circuitous path that ended almost exactly where it started.

It was originally built by the Ford Motor Company at its Wixom plant—roughly 30 miles northwest of the Henry Ford Museum—just as JFK was beginning his presidency in January 1961. It was then sent to Cincinnati, Ohio, to Hess & Eisenhardt, a well-respected coach-builder that was tasked with converting the car into the elaborate presidential parade vehicle it would become. At a cost of $200,000 (an eye-raising amount that becomes even more startling when you consider the retail price of a Lincoln Continental at the time was just over $7,300), the car was cut in half and extended three-and-a-half feet in length. Then it was souped up with state-of-the-art technology of the time: two radio telephones, a hydraulic lift on the rear seat, interior floodlights to illuminate the president at night, and three different kinds of detachable roofs (though none were bullet-proof). Painted a cool midnight blue, this presidential parade car represented a new look for a new decade and a dashing young president. It was delivered to the White House in June of '61 and given the Secret Service code name "X-100," which sounds ominous even without knowing its eventual role in history. But interestingly, it was never actually owned by the federal government. The Ford Motor Company leased the limousine to the Secret Service at the bargain-basement rate of $500 per year.

While the JFK limo remains one of the most popular attractions at the Henry Ford Museum, most visitors are only able to identify it with the help of the signage around it. And who can blame them, since the car looks absolutely nothing like it looked in Dallas. Today it looks like—and basically is—a completely different automobile because, to the surprise of those same visitors, the car in which the thirty-fifth president was brutally murdered actually stayed in service for *fourteen more years* after the assassination.

"People are just astonished when they learn that fact," Anderson says. "You would assume it would have been destroyed or locked up in a warehouse somewhere and never seen again."

Understandably, the X-100 was a key piece of evidence in the investigation that followed the president's murder. It was flown back

The Kennedy limousine—also known as the X-100—minutes before the shots rang out in Dealey Plaza (Jim Walker Collection/The Sixth Floor Museum at Dealey Plaza).

to Washington the night of November 22 and driven with a police escort to the White House garage, where it was impounded and remained under tight security for the next month. But once investigators were done examining it and Secret Service agents cleaned and repaired the car as best they could (though no amount of work could cover all the damage or remove the reminders of what had happened in it), the decision was made to revamp and retool it rather than take it out of commission.

Through the lens of history, it may seem callous (or perhaps even a bit ghoulish) to kick the Kennedy limousine back into play. But, then and now, the decision does make some manner of sense. To design and build a new car from scratch and then add all the additional security components that the assassination had prompted would take years and cost dramatically more than sprucing up the current car.

"It was even more about time savings than it was cost," Anderson said. "The president needed a parade limousine. And everything changed with the Kennedy assassination in terms of how a president was transported. They had to build an armored limousine that could be used by the president at any time. It was an absolute top priority to get that done and it was just faster at the end of the day to work with the car they already had rather than to start from scratch."

The plan to retool the limo—robotically classified, as these things seem to be, as "Project R-2," or more colloquially as "the quick fix"—was approved by the White House three weeks after the assassination. Ironically, the first stop in the revamp was the Engineering Research Division at Ford's Rouge Plant in, believe it or not, Dearborn, Michigan—basically a parking lot away from where the car now sits. It was then returned to Hess & Eisenhardt, where work began on what would become a $500,000 overhaul that replaced about 80 percent of the car.

More than 1,600 pounds of metal were added. That included a bullet-proof non-removable top anchored by a 1,500-pound, three-inch-thick rear window which, at the time, was the largest piece of curved bullet-resistant glass ever made. Naturally, the engine was also replaced with a more powerful one to account for all the extra weight. Also added was a new gas tank filled with urethane plastic foam that would minimize the possibility of an explosion, and aluminum inner tires to prevent flats if the car were fired on. But perhaps the most important change was the last one. After it was delivered the following summer, Lyndon Johnson—who, it was rumored, did whatever he could to avoid riding in that limo forever after—ordered that the car be repainted black from its original midnight blue color. He wanted to make sure no one ever recognized that car as *that* car.

And when you stand beside it at the Henry Ford Museum, you probably won't. It looks impressive and presidential to be sure, but you have to really hunker down and remind yourself that this is indeed the vehicle that Kennedy was shot in. That's because virtually none of its current visible pieces were part of the car in 1963. What marginal resemblance the limousine had to its original state after its quick fix was completely overhauled when it underwent another,

The refurbished (and essentially unrecognizable) Kennedy limousine on display at the Henry Ford Museum, just over 100 feet away from the Lincoln rocker (photograph by the author).

even more expansive remodel in 1967, during which it was stripped down to the bare metal and essentially entirely rebuilt.

Which leads one to naturally wonder what, if any, part of the car parked in the Henry Ford Museum today was in Dealey Plaza in 1963. "That's the million-dollar question, what is left of that car," Anderson says. "I'd honestly have to say it is the same car and is not the same car all at the same time. I don't think there's very much left except for the frame itself. Maybe a fender badge or something here or there." Thus the Kennedy limousine becomes a modern interpretation of the philosophical pondering of the ship of Theseus: whether an object that has gradually had each of its components replaced is, fundamentally, the same object.

In some ways, the fact that the car looks nothing like it did makes it being on display go down a little smoother. Anderson admits that to have refurbished the car to its original appearance would be in poor taste and likely take on a much more macabre flavor.

Still, if not reflected in physical accessories, the importance of the vehicle remains. Outside of its historical significance, it's a fuel-injected leviathan—23 feet long and weighing in at 10,000 pounds. And even if not immediately recognizable, it carries an undeniable gravitas. You can feel relevance radiating off it like waves of heat off parking-lot pavement on a summer afternoon. And in the visitor-friendly manner in which it's displayed, you can stand within inches of the car and truly inspect it, allowing yourself to consider what happened inside it. You can lean in and gaze through the windows on the passenger side to see the rear seat in which Kennedy was sitting when the shots were fired. Or rather, the seat that replaced the seat that replaced the seat in which Kennedy was sitting. But still.

And, if you're at just the right angle, you'll catch a perfect reflection of the vintage electric McDonald's sign which hangs just off to the side of the museum's presidential cars display. Gazing upon the exact spot where Kennedy sat, you can see a single, illuminated golden arch and Speedee, the chain's original cartoon mascot, with flashing lights providing the illusion of his legs moving at a rapid pace in order to deliver 15-cent hamburgers to a nation that desperately needed them. It's nothing more than an unintentional overlap of sight lines, of course. One part of the museum accidentally intruding on another, creating a conspicuous intersection of tone: perhaps the flimsiest and most insubstantial American experience set overtop one of America's most profound moments. Somehow it's funny, poignant, and perversely appropriate all at once.

After the Kennedy limousine was put back into service, presidents Johnson, Richard Nixon, Gerald Ford, and Jimmy Carter each used it, with hardly anyone ever knowing it was the same car which bore tragedy in Dallas. Though its use declined over the years. A newer, more cutting-edge limo entered the fleet in 1969 and the Kennedy limousine went from A car to B car. It's worth noting that it was not the car Ford was standing beside when would-be assassin Sara Jane Moore fired a shot at him in San Francisco in 1975. That was another limousine (though also a Lincoln Continental) which joined the presidential fleet in 1974.

The Kennedy car remained in use until it was officially retired in 1977 and joined the Henry Ford Museum the following year. Though it wasn't put on display until 1981, primarily because museum policy at the time was that any car under 20 years old wasn't considered quote-unquote historic. Today it's permanently parked along the east interior wall, right beside a horse-drawn carriage used by Theodore Roosevelt and other limousines used by FDR, Eisenhower, and Ronald Reagan. (Interestingly, the Reagan limo on display is the same one he was shot getting into in 1981, and which then rushed him to the hospital.)

If you turn your back on this parade of presidential hoopty and take a brisk stroll through the William Clay Ford Plaza of Innovation, you can make a sharp right turn into the "With Liberty and Justice for All" province of the Henry Ford Museum. Arguably the soul of the entire facility, visitors can explore insightful displays on civil rights and women's suffrage. They can see the camp bed George Washington slept in as he toured New York in 1783 and climb aboard the bus on which Rosa Parks declined a ridiculous offer to switch seats in 1955. But in the center of this section sits perhaps the signature piece of the entire museum: the surprisingly small velvet rocking chair in which Abraham Lincoln was shot.

The first thing that crosses your mind when you see the chair is a question you generally don't ask when you're on vacation.

Wait—is that blood?

In short, yes, there is blood on that chair, but no, what you think you see is not what you see.

Then what the heck is it? You subsequently may wonder. *That big dark patch across the top?*

You mean the pervasive stain that all logic suggests is the president's dried blood but actually isn't? We'll get to that in a minute, for it's a key part of the fascinating story behind the most famous piece of furniture in American history.

Prior to 10:15 p.m. on April 14, 1865, that rocking chair wasn't much more significant than the recliner that sits in your living room. In fact, just a few hours before the assassination, it was sitting in the bedroom of Harry Clay Ford, the owner of Ford's Theatre (and no direct relation to Henry Ford or, for that matter, the similarly named William Clay Ford). After learning that President Lincoln was planning to attend that night's performance of *Our American Cousin*, Ford dispatched a young employee named Joe Simms up to Fords' apartment across the alley from the theatre to bring the rocking chair to the presidential box. That Simms did, carrying it through the alley up above his head with the casual ease with which you'd haul patio furniture out of the garage.

The Lincoln rocker on display at the Henry Ford Museum (photograph by the author).

Still, even that afternoon, the chair held some manner of significance. It was the same chair Lincoln had sat in during several of his previous trips to Ford's Theatre: a Rococo Revival brown walnut rocker with red silk fabric that was actually part of a matching parlor suite Ford had purchased in 1863. Forty-two inches tall, just under 37 inches wide, and 34½ inches long. "It's not really a fancy chair, it's not really a cheap chair," says Charles Sable, Curator of Decorative Arts at the Henry Ford Museum. "It's sort of a middle-level chair that went along with a sofa and some other side chairs. It's nothing special. Those chairs were a dime a dozen in the 1860s. But it's not the chair, it's who sat in the damn chair. That's what's so important about it."

Yet even with that importance, it took quite a while for the chair to receive its due respect. While Kennedy's limousine took a rather straightforward path to Dearborn, joining the museum's collection less than a year after being retired from service and less than 15 years after the assassination, Lincoln's rocker took a much longer, more bizarre path.

Immediately after the assassination, both the theatre and the presidential box, with the furniture still in it, were sealed by authorities. Eight days later, Assistant Secretary of War Charles Dana ordered that the chair be removed from the box and stored as evidence for the eventual trial of the conspirators. After the trial was over, the chair sat in the office of Secretary of War Edwin Stanton for over a year, almost as a makeshift memorial to the fallen president. Eventually, the natural question emerged: what to do with this chair? And, while we're at it, the stovepipe hat that Lincoln had worn to the theatre that night, which would be the Sundance Kid to the chair's Butch Cassidy for the next half-century.

"They didn't really know what to do with them," says Harry Rubenstein, former Chair of the Division of Political History and Curator Emeritus at the Smithsonian. "But they knew they shouldn't get rid of them. So they transferred them to the Interior Department."

The transfer took place on August 7, 1866, exactly 13 months after Lincoln's conspirators had been hanged in public in front of paying spectators on a sweltering summer afternoon. The hat was subsequently put on display as part of a small historic exhibit at the U.S. Patent Office, where visitors could gaze upon it as a haunting reminder of what had happened that night. The chair, conversely, was not put on display. This would be a repeating trope over the coming years. An extremely fine line was drawn between the two relics: displaying the chair that Lincoln was sitting in when he was shot was considered ghoulish and in poor taste, but displaying the hat was not. So while the hat remained on display over the next year, the chair was packed away, out of sight. Why and where that line was drawn is, even today, a bit of a mystery—that there was a comfort level with the hat that did not carry over to the chair. Almost as if the chair were complicit in the assassination while the hat was just an innocent bystander.

Then the story takes a strange little turn.

For reasons that are still not entirely clear, in 1867 the chair and the hat were delivered to what one would assume would be their final destination: the Smithsonian Institution. But in a mind-blowing twist for what would become the most famous museum in America, the Smithsonian opted not to display either. In fact, the Secretary of the Smithsonian, Joseph Henry, ordered that both items be boxed up and hidden away—even the hat, which had just been on public display for over a year. And even more curious, he instructs his employees "not to mention the matter to any one, on account of there being so much excitement at the time." It was a somewhat cryptic comment, made all the more mysterious by his instruction to place both in a private storage room in the basement.

"It's hard to really know what went through Joseph Henry's mind at the time," Rubenstein says. "Was there something that happened that made them say, 'We should send these off to somebody who can take better care of them'? And maybe Henry just took them on to store them. That would be one possibility. The other is just Henry's personal feelings toward Lincoln. He was his science advisor and he knew the Lincolns. Therefore this personal relationship might have been enough for him to feel that (displaying them) was inappropriate.

"He accepts them and doesn't try to return them. But he also orders everybody not to mention these things. We don't know whether he's talking about the Civil War when he says 'so much excitement' or whether some incident happened when the hat was on display at the Patent Office."

It's also worth pointing out that the Smithsonian in 1867 was not the Smithsonian we know today. Upon its founding in 1846, it was more of a scientific institution than what we would think of as a museum. It wasn't until the United States centennial in 1876, when a large collection of historical artifacts was donated to the Smithsonian, that it began to evolve into a true museum. In 1867, displaying either the hat or the chair didn't seem to be a good idea, particularly, as in Henry's apparent view, that doing so would just draw curiosity seekers that would interrupt the work taking place at the Smithsonian.

So they sat in the basement, unseen, untouched, and unspoken of—for the next 26 years.

Then, in October of 1893, the hat was loaned to a museum run by Lincoln historian and collector Osborn Oldroyd (a fascinating character we'll get to know later) in what is now known as the Petersen House, just across the street from Ford's Theatre. For the next three years, the hat remained on display. When the museum closed in 1896, the hat was returned to the Smithsonian, and would officially be catalogued as part of the museum's collection in 1902. At that point, the hat was put on display, and remains so to this day, at the National Museum of American History. But the chair remained sealed off from public view. It was cataloged and considered an official part of the museum's collection, but for the next 30 years, remained secretly hidden away like the Ark of the Covenant in *Raiders of the Lost Ark*'s fictional Well of the Souls. Ironically, the person who released the chair from its inconspicuous resting place was Lincoln's Civil War adversary. Or his heirs, anyway.

After President of the Confederacy Jefferson Davis was captured at the end of the war, all of his belongings were seized by the U.S. government and remained in its possession well after Davis's death in 1889. In 1913, the Davis family contended that there was no legal basis for this action and demanded that the property be returned to the family. President Woodrow Wilson signed an executive order to release the items and the family regained possession after nearly 50 years.

In 1927, Blanche Chapman Ford, the widow of Harry Clay Ford, heard of the Davis family case. She wrote a letter to the Smithsonian asking the natural question we're asking ourselves: *If you have the chair Lincoln was shot in, why isn't it on display?* And, more to the point, *If you don't want it, may I please have it back?*

The answer to the first question, Smithsonian curator Theodore Belote wrote in his reply, was that it was museum policy not to show objects "directly connected with such a horrible and deplorable event."

It's difficult for our modern sensibilities to understand that explanation, 60-plus years after Lincoln's assassination. It would seem that the psychological wound would have healed enough by that point that displaying the chair wouldn't have been considered taboo. Though, by contrast, today the clothes JFK was wearing when he was shot, along with the infamous pink suit Jackie Kennedy wore that day, are both carefully stored in climate-controlled conditions at the National Archives and have never been displayed in the more than half-century since the assassination. Human nature being what it is, it's likely that both will see the light of day at some point, but for now, for many, it still feels inappropriate.

So when Mrs. Ford asked, with the request of the Davis descendants as precedent, if she could have the Lincoln chair back as it was rightly the property of her late husband, the Smithsonian put up no argument. And thus willingly gave up one of the most fascinating artifacts in American history.

"The reason for giving it back does not hold up," Rubenstein admits. "But there was the whole question about appropriateness, and Mrs. Ford had a reasonable claim. If we wanted to keep it, we would have had to make a counterclaim and go to court. At that point in time, something like that wasn't going to be used, so it was just easier to say 'Let's not even bother.'"

So, in the spring of 1929, Mrs. Ford's son George picked up the chair and returned it to his mother. Whether she genuinely wanted the chair or always intended to turn around and sell it is unclear. (Though, it's worth noting, the stock market crash that prompted the onset of the Great Depression occurred six months after she acquired it and could have factored into the decision.) Just before Christmas, she put the chair up for auction with Anderson Galleries in New York.

It caught the attention of many potential buyers, but none more than legendary antiques dealer Israel Sack. He had no intention of acquiring it for himself, but like Mrs. Ford and Osborn Oldroyd before him, saw a way to profit from it. He bought it for $2,400 and turned right around to offer it for sale to someone he knew would be immensely interested in it: Henry Ford, who had just opened a new museum in Michigan. Ford, an admirer of Lincoln, had already acquired the historic Logan County Courthouse where Lincoln had practiced law early in his career in Illinois, and had it moved to Dearborn, restored, and opened to the public.

In January 1930, the chair was delivered to Ford, who, unlike the Smithsonian, was so enchanted by its historical significance that he had the unpacking of the chair filmed. The museum has transferred the grainy, black-and-white film to a digital file and posted it on its YouTube channel. It's essentially just a clip of two guys unpacking a chair from a large wooden box—not unlike Ralphie's dad unveiling his cherished leg lamp in *A Christmas Story*. After almost two minutes of watching these guys who had no idea they'd one day become internet stars muscle through an almost comical amount of packing material, the chair is finally unveiled, looking much as it does today. Then, the older guy who looks a lot like Boo Radley casually picks it up with his bare hands and meanders offscreen with it as if repositioning a lawn chair at a barbecue. Slapstick as this little film looks to our modern eyes, knowing how long it took for the chair to finally receive the historical appreciation it deserved makes the film both interesting and more than a bit haunting.

The chair was put on display in the refurbished Logan County Courthouse (which Ford had turned into a shrine to Lincoln) in Greenfield Village, and there it spent the next half century. In 1979, it was moved to the primary museum as part of its fiftieth-anniversary celebration. Then in the mid–1990s, the chair was conserved—the fabric stabilized and the wood carefully cleaned—and placed in a climate-controlled glass case.

There it resides today, in the aorta of the Henry Ford Museum. Thousands of visitors gaze upon it each year and crinkle their noses at what they believe is a massive dark patch of blood at the top of the upholstery—presumably the final remnants of the Great Emancipator that soaked into the chair, as if baptizing it into history.

After "where are the bathrooms," it's perhaps the museum's most frequently asked question. "I don't know how many times we get asked about the blood," Sable says. "Everybody wants to know about the darn blood. And it ain't blood."

It's true. For as much as it looks like it, and as much as you'd expect it to be considering the terrible history of this particular piece of furniture, it's not blood that marks the top of that rocking chair. Not Lincoln's and not anyone else's.

The big ugly stain across the top of the chair is ... drumroll, please ... hair oil.

Primarily hair oil, anyway, with some water damage and dried plaster dust mixed in. All of which reflects the ultra-casual attitude that was taken with the chair before it wound up in Dearborn.

The rocking chair Abraham Lincoln was shot in as it appeared just after the assassination, before being hidden away for nearly a century (Library of Congress).

In fact, the oil stains dated back to well before the time when Lincoln's rocking chair became an historic item and was subsequently stuffed in a damp basement like a broken ping-pong table. That's where it suffered most of its weathering. "It took a beating in the Smithsonian," Sable says. "If you look at the stereoscope images of it from 1865 and then look at the 1920s images of it—oh my gosh, that poor chair."

Harry Ford had originally purchased the chair and the suite that came with it to place in a reception room at the theatre. Ushers would often relax in the chair when they weren't working, and it didn't take long for the greasy oil applied to their generally unwashed hair to begin to saturate the silk damask fabric on the headrest portion of the rocker. It's possible that some of that residue may have come from Lincoln himself, since he began using the chair whenever he would come to the theatre. But because of his height, it's more likely that his head never touched that part of the chair, therefore the president probably did not contribute to the eternal stain.

On the other hand, his notable height was one of the reasons the president really liked this chair. "We knew he used it whenever he came to Ford's Theatre because he found it so comfortable," Sable says. "It was just the shape of the rocker that he liked. He fit into it very comfortably." Accordingly, each time Lincoln would come to the theatre, Ford would dispatch an employee to bring the rocker up to the box for the president to sit in during the performance. With the chair more or less known, at least within Ford's Theatre, as the "president's rocker," in 1864, Ford had the chair moved to his apartment to try to preserve it and protect it from further stains or damage. Nearly two centuries later, we can see that was a fruitless endeavor.

For anyone with a taste for the morbid, rest assured there are indeed some traces of blood on the chair. During the conservation efforts in the '90s, testing concluded there were traces at the front of the seat and near the upper portion of the back. Though it hasn't been scientifically proven (and likely won't, since there's virtually no samples of DNA to use as a match) and knowing that the president's head wound actually bled very little, it's still possible that at least some of the blood on that chair belonged to Lincoln.

Lest we forget, however, Lincoln's was not the only blood shed in the presidential box that fateful night. Nor was Kennedy the only man shot in the X-100. For in yet another of the more curious coincidences between the two murders, each president and his wife were accompanied by another couple. And each of those other women witnessed her companion seriously wounded and subsequently forever etched into history simply for being in the wrong place at the wrong time.

6

A Haunted Dress and
the Shadow of History

Without question, they were the worst two double dates ever.

One was a trip to the theatre, the other a drive across town for lunch. Each venture ended in death for one gentleman in the quartet and near-fatal injuries for the other. Both pairs of women went home covered in blood, and bystanders suffered emotional scars that would never completely heal. Only Stephen King's *Carrie* could offer a comparably disastrous outing.

Which isn't to make light of what happened in both cases, but rather to underline one of the often-mentioned but less-appreciated coincidences between the Lincoln and Kennedy assassinations. That both men were not only in the presence of their wives, but that the first couple was sitting alongside another couple at the fateful moment.

Of course, there are innumerable presidential events—state dinners, ceremonies, and the like—in which the commander in chief is joined by his wife in a formal setting. In some of these, they may whisk through the evening alongside another couple of note: a visiting dignitary from another country, for example. But that's not what either of these events were. They were relative aberrations, logistical pairings that would have been considered fairly unusual and unique in both the 1860s and 1960s.

That both presidents would be assassinated while a part of the exact same social lineup is pretty remarkable. Again, looking back to our assassination control group, neither Garfield nor McKinley had similar accompaniment, to say nothing of the exact same cast of characters. Their wives were nowhere in the vicinity, even though, in theory, they could have been. Garfield was catching a train for a trip out of Washington and McKinley was at an event greeting the public. It would have made sense had either or both of their wives been with them, but that neither actually was reflects the uniqueness of Mrs. Lincoln and Mrs. Kennedy's presence.

Still, the similar supporting casts in both the Lincoln and Kennedy assassinations are little more than footnote material. You often see details about the wounds of the president's wingmen and a couple of memorable one-liners they cried out as tragedy struck. Very little is said by historians and even less is remembered by the general populace about the truly fascinating lives of the men who were sitting alongside the doomed presidents at the moment of tragedy: Major Henry Rathbone and Governor John Connally.

If either remains in the zeitgeist with greater illumination, it's Connally. Not only because, thanks to the Zapruder film, he had more of an imminent visual role in the event, but because he was, both before and after the assassination, a much more vibrant and

Despite a long and distinguished political career, John Connally would primarily be remembered for nearly dying alongside President Kennedy on the day of the assassination (Library of Congress).

historically impactful character. Who very nearly became president himself.

Let's start with what he's remembered most for. In the frantic seconds of confusion as the shots began to ring out in Dealey Plaza, Connally recognized exactly what was happening. An experienced hunter, he was able to define the sound of rifle fire while many others had mistaken it for a firecracker or motorcycle backfire.

After the first shot, which missed, Connally turned in the jump seat just ahead of Kennedy in the X-100, craning his neck to try to figure out what was going on. As he did, the second shot struck Kennedy in the throat and continued on a downward path that would stitch Connally much more permanently into the narrative. The same bullet entered Connally's back, clipping the end of his fifth rib and collapsing his right lung. It then exited through his chest just beneath the nipple. It continued straight through Connally's right wrist, shattering his radius bone, then buried itself in his left thigh. His wounds—five in all—were serious, but had he not turned in his seat the moment before, the bullet almost certainly would have gone directly through his heart, likely killing him on the spot.

It all happened in a second. As Connally felt immense pain as the bullet ripped through his body, he looked down and saw blood pouring onto his shirt. Certain he was about to die, he shouted, "My God! They're going to kill us all!"

As he cavorted in pain, his wife Nellie became aware of what was happening. She pulled Connally down into her lap and tried to soothe him as the limousine raced toward Parkland Hospital, telling him everything was going to be all right. And for Connally, at least, it was. After several hours of surgery that afternoon, doctors were confident Connally would survive with little or no lasting damage. Part of the reason he got off fairly lucky was that because of Nellie pulling him down, his arm covered the baseball-sized sucking wound in his chest and prevented additional air from escaping his damaged lung. Had this serendipitous arrangement of appendages not occurred, Connally may have died in his wife's lap as the limousine raced down Stemmons Freeway. As it was, twice during the five-minute journey to the hospital, Nellie thought her husband had died.

In addition to the physical damage done, Connally had to work through psychological aftereffects. He remained primarily unconscious through most of the weekend that followed the assassination. When he finally awoke on Monday, Nellie had to carefully explain everything that had happened: the president's death and impending funeral that afternoon in Washington. And while the alleged assassin had been captured, he'd subsequently been gunned down in public the previous morning. Connally, still a bit woozy, could understandably not quite comprehend all he was hearing or even what exactly had happened to him. Indeed, for a long period afterward, Connally would have sludgy, sweaty nightmares that always ended with him getting shot in different scenarios.

While he never doubted the conclusion of the Warren Commission that Oswald acted alone, he opened himself up to a curious contradiction that provided fodder for conspiracy theorists for years. He always contended his belief that he was hit by a separate bullet than the one that caused Kennedy's neck wound. Which, if true, would have to lead to the conclusion of two different shooters—which Connally made clear he did not believe nor endorse. Even his infamous exclamation at the moment of the shooting, "*They're* going to kill us all," has been held up by some as evidence that Connally knew this wasn't solely the work of a minimum-wage warehouse employee.

Often lost to history was that Connally was essentially the master of ceremonies for Kennedy's swing through Texas. While the primary purpose of the trip was a pre-campaign fundraising swing through a critical state in the next presidential election, now less than a year away, another reason was to resolve a childish political squabble among the leadership within the Texas Democratic Party. Connally was at the vanguard of the state's conservative Democratic wing, while Senator Ralph Yarborough shored up the state party's more liberal faction. The two couldn't stand each other. Truth be told, Connally also wasn't crazy about JFK, who was far too East Coast elite for his taste, and feared a backlash from his base for chumming around the state with the liberal-leaning president. Partially for this reason, Connally had postponed the trip several times before it was finalized that June. He then pushed for a smaller itinerary rather than the four-cities-in-two-days whirlwind it became.

Though he had previously served in the Kennedy administration, Connally was a Lyndon Johnson man through and through, having been associated with LBJ for nearly a quarter century at that point. He'd been a friend and aide for Johnson early in both men's careers, and ran Johnson's halfhearted campaign for president in 1960 until the nomination went to Kennedy. When Johnson was selected as the running mate, Connally came along for the ride and helped secure Texas for the Kennedy-Johnson ticket. As a reward, Johnson convinced Kennedy to appoint Connally as secretary of the Navy. He only served in the role for a year before resigning to return to Texas to run for governor.

Just after he resigned as secretary, he received what at the time appeared like nothing more than an ordinary letter from a former Marine. But in retrospect, it's a slice of creepy, cryptic foreshadowing that is often not given its due. In February 1962, some 21 months before he would nearly be killed on a drive through downtown Dallas, John Connally received a letter from the man who would shoot him.

At the time, Lee Harvey Oswald was living in Russia, having defected in the fall of 1959, and was trying to return to the United States. When he'd left the Marines, he'd received an honorable discharge, but after he defected to Russia, it was changed to an "undesirable" discharge (slightly different from and not quite as serious as a "dishonorable" discharge). It would be nearly a year and a half before Oswald learned of the change, and once he did, he wrote to Connally to ask him to shift the designation back.

Considering what would eventually happen and how these two men would be connected, it's an eerie little letter. Oswald opens by noting a benign personal connection, that they'd both been residents of Fort Worth. He then passes off his defection to the Soviet Union as no big deal, comparing himself to Ernest Hemingway, explaining that his defection to Russia was just like the great writer moving to Paris for a short while. He also told Connally that he would "employ all means to right this gross mistake or injustice." While there's no threatening language in the letter, the signature of "Thank you, Lee H. Oswald" is enough to provide a little shiver.

Oswald, of course, didn't realize that Connally was no longer the secretary of the Navy, having resigned to run for governor six weeks earlier at the time the letter was sent. Connally said he never saw the letter, and it was simply forwarded to his successor. A cold form letter explaining this was sent back to Oswald, whose request was ultimately declined.

Admittedly, aside from being unsettling, there doesn't appear to be much to this tale—basically the postal equivalent of dialing a wrong number. Connally hadn't been secretary when Oswald's discharge was changed, and he was no longer secretary when Oswald's request was denied. To any reasonable person, Connally did nothing that could have angered Oswald. But it's not going out on a limb to state that Oswald was not a reasonable man. It's possible he still may have projected his anger about the whole thing onto Connally, and that, combined with Connally's well-known anti-communist stance, may have propelled Oswald's actions. Connally himself admitted years later he always wondered if that terse response to Oswald's request may have planted the seed that eventually led to the assassination.

When the letter came to light, investigators considered the possibility that it was Connally that was Oswald's actual target that day in Dallas. Even Oswald's wife Marina testified to the Warren Commission that she initially thought that her husband was shooting at Connally rather than Kennedy. This line of thinking sputters out pretty quickly, but since Oswald also never appeared to show any ill will or animosity toward President Kennedy, it remains on the periphery of any debate about his true objective.

There was one final coincidence connecting the assassin and his apparently accidental victim. After Oswald was shot by Jack Ruby while in police custody, he was rushed to Parkland Hospital and wheeled into the same examination room—Trauma Room 2—where Connally had been treated 48 hours before.

Connally recovered from his wounds and went on to a distinguished political career, though everything he accomplished always seemed to be subordinate in people's minds to his actual legacy. Fittingly, he titled his autobiography *In History's Shadow*, an oblique admission that he would always be remembered first and foremost for what happened on November 22, 1963.

Still, the 30 years of his life that followed were quite a journey. He went on to serve as governor of Texas for six years, being re-elected twice to two-year terms by a wide margin. While still a Democrat, his conservative track made him appealing across the aisle, and in 1971, he was appointed Secretary of the Treasury by Richard Nixon. Connally resigned the position a year later, then headed up a group called Democrats for Nixon as the president ramped up his successful bid for reelection. But Nixon also had his eye beyond his second term, and, beginning to see himself in the kingmaker role, saw Connally as the perfect successor, even though Connally was still a Democrat.

In fact, Nixon even reportedly considered replacing Spiro Agnew with Connally as his running mate on the '72 ticket. Nixon ultimately stuck with Agnew, but again was drawn to Connally when Agnew was forced to resign over a tax evasion and bribery scandal in 1973. By now Connally had officially switched party affiliation from Democrat to Republican and had worked for Nixon as an unpaid advisor during the Watergate investigation. While he wasn't in the thick of the "cancer on the presidency" conversations taking place (and being recorded) around this time, his most memorable piece of advice was telling Nixon to set fire to all of the secret tapes of his White House conversations after they were revealed, potential obstruction of justice charges be damned.

Pyrotechnic guidance aside, Nixon wanted to select Connally as his new vice president after Agnew slunk back home to Maryland in disgrace. But as rumors of the idea spread, a sudden and fierce bloc of opposition arose in Congress. Democrats were still furious over Connally's party switch, and Republicans didn't quite trust him the way Nixon did. For Connally to get the job, a fierce battle would need to be fought, which Nixon couldn't afford in the midst of the Watergate chess match already under way in the House of Representatives.

Nixon instead pivoted away from Connally and chose the more middle-of-the-road Gerald Ford as a slice of buttered toast to help ease America's upset stomach. But in so doing, Nixon explained to Ford that he'd be supporting Connally for president in the 1976 election. Which was fine with Ford, who had no intention of running himself.

At the time, no one could know how close Connally had come to actually becoming president. Less than a year after being named vice president, Ford assumed the presidency when Nixon resigned. Had Nixon gone with his initial instinct either time he considered replacing Spiro Agnew, Connally might have become president a decade after nearly dying alongside one.

Still, seemingly no relationship with Richard Milhaus Nixon in the early 1970s could end without getting tainted by scandal. Connally got his share in 1974 when he was indicted by a federal grand jury on charges of perjury and conspiracy to obstruct justice—not for anything directly connected to Watergate, but rather something much less sexy. And much more bovine.

While Treasury Secretary, he'd allegedly taken a $10,000 bribe from American Milk Producers Inc. for persuading Nixon to support an increase in dairy price supports in 1971. Connally was exonerated of the charge in 1975. The details were a bit fuzzy and his innocence wasn't quite crystal clear, but Connally ultimately proved he didn't have milk on his hands.

Connally had one last, albeit brief chapter in his political journey when he launched a bid for the Republican nomination for the presidency in 1979. He promptly dropped out of the race once he got his clock cleaned by Ronald Reagan in the South Carolina primary—his earlier president-in-the-wings status tainted by the stink of sour milk and his strong political connections to both Lyndon Johnson and Richard Nixon. Ultimately, his year-long presidential campaign resulted in spending $11 million and picking up just one delegate. Connally faded into retirement, but emerged in the news again a decade later when he declared bankruptcy after amounting more than $90 million in debt after a series of bad investment decisions.

Even though the reach of his political aspirations exceeded his grasp, his imprint is felt throughout Texas even today. An interstate highway, a hospital, a high school, and, for some reason, a wing of a correctional facility are named in his honor, and a statue of him stands in the posh Connally Plaza in downtown Houston. He died in 1993 at the age of 76, survived by his colorful wife Nellie, to whom he'd been married for 53 years.

While John Connally earned his own chapter of assassination lore, it was Nellie who holds claim to an equally memorable bit of trivia. As the limousine made its fateful turn onto Elm Street for the final leg of the parade, Nellie commented to Kennedy, "Well, Mr. President, you can't say Dallas doesn't love you." To which the president responded, "No, you certainly can't." Not only was it a bit of darkly ironic commentary just before the shots rang out, but also the last words Kennedy ever spoke.

Nellie's strength and support as she stayed by her husband's side is another rarely mentioned subplot of November 22, as is a chilling little tale from a few weeks after the assassination. When Nellie made a trip to the salon, her hairdresser prepared to begin his work but stopped and began closely examining the back of Nellie's head. The hairdresser let out a low whistle. "Mrs. Connally," he said, "did you know there is a streak of white hair, two inches wide, down the back of your head?" A startled Nellie had no idea—she'd never seen it and it hadn't been there the last time she'd been to the salon.

She quickly made an appointment with her family doctor to see what could have caused such a thing. "Shock," her doctor explained. "From what you say, you never screamed or even cried until after the event. You kept everything inside. That's what happens to good little soldiers."

It was as if the assassination had left a supernatural imprint, akin to something out of a horror story. Which was not unlike the fate of Nellie Connally's counterpart in the Lincoln assassination.

***

Clara Harris wasn't supposed to go to Ford's Theatre that night. Neither was her fiancé, Major Henry Rathbone. The couple was a last resort for the Lincolns, the seventh option to be invited to accompany them to see the drawing room farce *Our American Cousin*. In fact, Clara and Henry had received the offer only about two hours before the Lincolns' carriage arrived to pick them up. Two hours after that, Clara Harris and Henry Rathbone would be forever cemented in history.

Originally, it was supposed to be Ulysses Grant for what would have been the political equivalent of a victory lap. The triumphant general and toast of the victorious Union was in Washington that week and had initially been invited, along with his wife, to join the president and Mary Todd Lincoln at the theatre that Friday night. It had been announced in the Washington papers that Grant and Lincoln would attend the play together, and Harry Clay Ford, owner of Ford's Theatre, had an ad printed in the papers that afternoon carrying the news, in the hope of increasing attendance for that night's show. Interestingly, Grant's appearance would have been even more appealing than Lincoln's. Not only was Grant at the apex of his popularity, having just accepted Robert Lee's surrender to end the war five days earlier, but he was rarely seen in Washington, making him more of a mythic figure, conducting epic victories on distant battlefields.

That Friday afternoon, following a meeting with Lincoln and his cabinet, Grant informed the president that he and his wife would be leaving Washington early to visit their children in New Jersey. Thus, they couldn't attend the play. Disappointed but understanding, Lincoln bade his victorious general farewell for the final time. It leaves us with the first of several "what ifs" in Lincoln assassination lore. What if Grant had accompanied Lincoln as planned? Would things have unfolded differently—either for better or worse? Perhaps Grant's superior military acumen would have somehow enabled him to sniff out Booth's plot and stop it. Or, more likely, Grant might have been killed as well, giving Booth a BOGO assassination possibility. In an interesting historical footnote, Lincoln and Grant had attended a performance at Ford's Theatre together just two months earlier. Another what-if possibility poses that Grant would have been accompanied by a military guard on April 14 (though, with or without Grant, Lincoln would not have been so accompanied—nineteenth-century security practices tend to be hilarious compared to today's). Therefore, the theory goes, Booth wouldn't have been able to get into the box in the first place. But Grant was actually not accompanied by guards on his trip to the theatre in February, so it's safe to assume he wouldn't have been this time around, either. Still, the alternate way things might have played out with Grant in the box is a fascinating doorway.

With Grant's thanks/no thanks, the Lincolns could have cancelled. Without the symbolism of Lincoln and Grant out on the town together basking in the glow of snuffed-out secession, the trip to the theatre now lost much of its appeal. Based on comments both had made throughout that Friday, it seems neither Lincoln nor Mary were particularly excited about going to the show that night. But since his appearance had been ballyhooed in the papers, Lincoln felt obligated to go to prevent theatregoers from feeling gypped.

So, in what became its own drawing room farce, the backup planning began. Indiana representative Schuyler Colfax—who, ironically, would become Ulysses Grant's vice president four years later—was invited, but was leaving for a trip to the West Coast and declined. Reporter Noah Brooks, a friend of the Lincolns, was fighting off a cold. The Lincolns' own son, Robert Todd, turned down the offer for a good night's sleep after having spent the past several weeks traveling the front with Grant. An invitation was extended to the Marquis Adolphe de Chambrun, a visiting French diplomat, who declined on the grounds that it was Good Friday, and attending the theatre felt inappropriate. With time running short, Edwin Stanton, Lincoln's secretary of war, turned down his invitation primarily because he didn't want the president to attend either, for security reasons, and hoped this final decline would convince Lincoln to stay home.

It's easy to look at this long line of regrets in retrospect and theorize that fate was nudging Abraham Lincoln to stay home. But the president was determined to see the show and be seen by its audience.

With just a few hours until the curtain, Stanton's turn-down led the Lincolns to Clara Harris and Henry Rathbone. Mary and Clara had become good friends over the previous four years. Both had arrived in Washington at the same time—Mary joining her husband as he began his presidency and Clara accompanying her father Ira Harris, who'd been appointed New York senator to replace William Seward when he resigned from the position to become Lincoln's secretary of state. Clara often visited Mary at the White House and would accompany her on other trips to the theatre or opera. In fact, Clara had been at Mary's side three nights earlier when Lincoln gave his final speech from the White House balcony to revelers below.

Perhaps not knowing quite how much of a last resort they were, Clara and Henry enthusiastically accepted, leading to yet another what if: had they also declined, the Lincolns likely would have been out of options. Not wanting to attend alone (for the optics if nothing else), they might have finally determined that going to the play was a bad idea. Would one more declined invitation have saved Abraham Lincoln's life?

Though it's difficult to imagine Clara and Henry declining. Not only was Clara good friends with Mary, but Henry was an ambitious young military officer who'd led troops in several battles during the war, including Antietam. To be seen out in public as the president's guest, even if no one knew who you were, would be quite a coup. Indeed, as they

Major Henry Rathbone was a last-minute theatre guest of the Lincolns on the night of the assassination and would be tortured by what happened there for the rest of his life (National Archives).

entered the theatre with the president and first lady, the play stopped. The audience offered the arriving guests a rousing round of applause as they marched across the dress circle toward their reserved seats in the presidential box while the orchestra played "Hail to the Chief." While the crowd was likely still expecting General Grant and wondering just who this mystery couple was, this moment of recognition likely was a defining moment for them both: dark complexioned and beautiful Clara at 30 and dashing, mutton-chopped Henry at 27, both young and happy with a life laid out before them on a golden track. The Lincolns' invitation was the perfect offer at the perfect time. Which leads us to the generally uncomfortable story of Clara and Henry's romance.

They were brought together by the same thing that ultimately makes them a part of history: death. Growing up with similarly well-to-do families in Albany, New York, Henry's father and Clara's mother died within days of each other. The widow and widower, who'd traveled in the same social circles, found one another in their grief and were married three years later. Thus, Clara, age thirteen, and Henry, age eleven, moved into the same house and grew up together as stepbrother and stepsister—though some accounts suggest that they considered themselves more like cousins. Which doesn't really make it better.

Be that as it may, they were drawn to one another, exchanging letters while Henry was away at school. When Henry returned to Washington after suffering from illness during the war, he was able to spend more time with Clara. They became engaged a few months before the trip to the theatre and were about to set a date for their wedding.

As you wince a bit and shift in your seat while mulling over the backstory, let's correct a common optical misconception about the assassination. In most illustrations depicting Booth's shooting of Lincoln, the quartet of spectators are lined up in a row: Lincoln on the far right, Mary to his right, then Clara and Henry on the far left, often shown raising his arm in belated warning (and in a military uniform, though Henry was dressed in civilian clothes and unarmed that night). In reality, the seating arrangement in the box at Ford's

Theatre was much less linear. Lincoln and his wife were side by side on the far right, true. But in the cramped box (cramped *two* boxes actually—the partition between Box 7 and 8 had been removed that afternoon so all four could be in the same space), there wasn't enough room for Henry and Clara to sit beside one another parallel to the Lincolns. Clara sat in a chair beside Mary, but there wasn't room for Henry to sit beside his fiancé. He was actually sitting behind her on a small couch pushed at an angle against the back wall of the box, barely able to see the stage at all. This detail is less about correcting the artistic renditions of the assassination than to spotlight a potentially important logistical aspect that may help explain Henry Rathbone's ultimate fate.

Like Nellie Connally's non sequitur about Dallas loving JFK just before it killed him, Clara Harris also factored into the final words her doomed president would hear. In an unusual moment of intimacy, Mary Todd Lincoln took her husband's hand and whispered to him, "What will Miss Harris think of my hanging on to you so?" To which the president replied his final words: "She won't think a thing about it."

The murder then unfolds—Booth entering the box under the auditory veil of the audience laughing at the play's funniest line and firing a single shot into the back of Lincoln's head. Hearing the shot, Henry leaps up to stop him, grappling with the assassin as the single-shot revolver clatters to the floor of the box. Booth whips out a long hunting knife and slices at Henry, who raises his left arm in defense. The blade slices through Henry's suit and carves open his arm between the elbow and the armpit, cutting all the way to the bone, and driving Henry to the floor.

Still holding the bloody knife, Booth climbs onto the ledge of the balcony, preparing to jump onto the stage. Henry gets up off the floor and makes one final lunge at Booth with his uninjured right arm. It's possible that Henry's last grasp may have knocked Booth off balance as he jumped, and caused him to land on the stage awkwardly and break his leg—an injury that, as we'll see later, not only altered Booth's escape plan but also played a key role in his ultimately getting caught. Another version of the story is that the spur of Booth's boot got caught in part of the American flag bunting that decorated the presidential box, and that's what caused him to jump awkwardly—the Revenge of Old Glory theory. Of course, it's also possible that neither version is true (jumping from a height of nine feet onto a hard wooden floor will often result in injury) or that both versions are true (perhaps Henry's final grab *caused* Booth's boot to get caught in the bunting).

Whatever the cause and effect, Booth leapt to the stage as Henry shouted, "Stop that man!" As he'd done countless times before, Booth stood in the center of the stage with all eyes in the theatre fixed upon him. He held aloft the knife drenched with Henry's blood and shouted to the audience unaware of what had just happened, "Sic semper tyranus!" Virginia's bizarre state motto, meaning, "Thus always for tyrants." Booth then rushed backstage and out of the theatre, leaving devastation in his wake. It was Clara who delivered the news to the still-confused audience, screaming, "The president's been shot!" and sending Ford's Theatre into pandemonium.

Henry, bleeding profusely, staggered to the entrance of the box, pushed away a plank of wood Booth had lodged between the door and the wall, and allowed help to enter the box. Clara did what she could for Henry, eventually wrapping his wound with a handkerchief to try to control the bleeding, which had drenched the floor of the box as well as Clara's dress. Like Nellie Connally would do with her husband a century later, Clara remained calm and did what she could to comfort her wounded fiancé.

The couple escorted Mary as Lincoln's body was carefully carried out of the theatre and onto rainy Tenth Street. They followed as the president was taken across the street to the Petersen House and stayed in the front parlor with Mary as visitors attended to Lincoln in the back bedroom. At one point, the distraught Mary noticed the condition of Clara's dress and cried out, "My husband's blood!" In reality, the blood was Henry's, not that of the president, who actually bled very little.

As the night went on, Henry continued to lose blood, resisting medical assistance so as not to deny any attention from the president. Henry became pale and light-headed, eventually passing out and lying unconscious on the hallway floor between the parlor and the back bedroom. Finally, a carriage was summoned and Henry and Clara were sent back to Senator Harris's house, where an Army surgeon sewed Henry's wound. Certainly, Henry's injury was much worse than he'd let them believe, and he very nearly died. It would be months before he regained use of his left arm, and it would never be the same again.

Nor would his mental state. Henry developed a deep sense of guilt over Lincoln's death, feeling he could have done more to save the president. This was combined with the embarrassment that he, a decorated military officer, couldn't stop or apprehend a mere actor from killing Lincoln and very nearly Henry himself. Much, if not all, of this was psychosomatic. There's no record of Henry being overtly blamed, either by the newspapers or to his face, though just the recognition Henry did receive seemed to be enough. Even without malice, people knew Henry as the man who failed to stop Booth. In the parlance of the theatre where the tragedy had taken place, Henry had been typecast by historical circumstance, and could never be recognized or remembered for anything else. He would be shrouded, even more than John Connally, by history's shadow. No one blamed Henry, and most saw him as a tragic figure who did his best. But Henry, always a bit of a melancholic character to begin with, was deeply infected with a guilt that would psychologically cripple him for the rest of his life.

Part of the reason for this mental self-flagellation may be rooted in the seating arrangement in the box. Sitting on the couch against the back wall rather than along the railing with the rest of the party, Henry was the closest person to Booth when he entered the box. He likely noticed him come through the door just beside— not behind—him and saw everything unfold. Based on his position and poor view of the stage, the likelihood is pretty high that Henry watched Booth step forward and shoot Lincoln, rather than the commonly accepted detail that he was unaware of anything happening until he heard the shot. This may well be the dream-like horror that played over and over in his mind for the rest of his life: the greatest tragedy in American history happening seven feet in front of him and he not able to act fast enough to prevent it.

Another possibility that could explain his personal torture is reflected in Clara's original account of what happened. At the Petersen House that night, she told an inquiring Secretary of War Edwin Stanton that Booth had actually first come into the box about an hour previously. He took a quick look around, then turned and left. When he returned the second time, Henry stood up and confronted him, asking him what he was doing. But Booth simply brushed past him and shot the president right in front of him. After Henry provided his affidavit to investigators a few days later, he didn't share this version of the story—potentially out of embarrassment—and Clara followed by telling a version that matched his: no earlier visit from Booth, no attempt to stop him at the door on the second encounter. Perhaps she wanted to adhere to Henry's version to prevent historical infamy, or maybe her original story was incorrect or misreported. Either way, even if it reached an irrational level, Henry's guilt can be understood.

In the aftermath, Henry and Clara did what they could to live the life they'd always intended. They were married two years later and would have three children, the first of whom was born in 1870 on Lincoln's birthday—a subtle, darkly ironic reminder that wasn't lost on either of them. That same year, Henry resigned from the Army and would never again hold a regular job, instead living on his family's wealth. It was around this time that Henry's behavior started to become noticeably odd. He would unnaturally steer conversations to the assassination and started to show signs of paranoia, primarily over Clara taking the children and leaving him. He slept with a loaded revolver under his pillow.

Suffering from constant headaches, he continued to descend into depression over the next decade, even as his family burgeoned and lived a seemingly charmed life. They'd travel through Europe each winter and return to Washington for summers of social occasions and relaxation. At one point, Henry tried to get a job in the administration of Rutherford Hayes, but he was unable to, even with impressive recommendations. His strange behavior and declining personality may ultimately have been the preventative factor. Modern analysis almost unilaterally concludes that Henry was suffering from a form of post-traumatic stress disorder, which today could be treated with counseling and medication. But in the nineteenth century, his condition, even if its origin was understood, was a complete mystery and became a lifelong burden.

As he became increasingly distant and difficult, Clara considered leaving him—likely only fueling his growing paranoia. Two days before Christmas in 1883, as the family was staying in Germany, Clara heard Henry arise before dawn and enter their children's bedroom down the hall. She followed to see him standing over their sleeping children, holding a revolver and a knife. He explained that he knew she was going to leave him and take the children, and this was the only way he could stop her. She managed to guide him back into their bedroom, where she tried to allay his fears and convince him it was all in his mind. It was no use.

Henry raised the gun and shot her twice in the chest, then stabbed her in the heart. He then turned the knife and stabbed himself five times, puncturing his lung. Whether consciously or not, Henry had mirrored John Wilkes Booth's actions in the presidential box: shooting one person and stabbing another. Clara's sister Louise, living with the family at the time, entered the room and found the couple lying on the bloody floor. She leaned down to her dying sister, who whispered, "He has killed us both at last." Henry, only semi-conscious, pulled himself up and looked upon his mortally wounded wife. "Who could have done this?" he cried, apparently unaware of what had just happened. "I have no enemies." Clara died shortly after, and as Henry was taken away by police, he warned them about the men hiding behind the paintings on the walls of the house.

His mind finally broken, Henry claimed to have no memory of killing Clara, instead explaining that someone had broken into the house and attacked his wife and then him when he tried to interfere. He was sent to an asylum for the criminally insane in Hildesheim, Germany, where he would spend the rest of his life. Still, his mental troubles never allayed. He worried the other inmates were conspiring against him. He heard voices, saw specters, and would often tell visitors about the machine built inside the walls that sprayed gas into his room which caused his recurring headaches. He died in 1911 at the age of 74 and was buried beside Clara at a cemetery in Hanover.

They rested in peace until 40 years later. When renewal fees to the cemetery came due for their plots, either no surviving family members were made aware or none thought to proceed with paying the dues—for even in death, it seems, we still owe rent. Thus, as was the cemetery's policy, Henry and Clara's bodies were exhumed and their headstones removed. A myth abounded for many years that their remains were simply disposed of, but further research determined that in fact the couple is still buried in the same spots. Deeper graves were excavated in the same locations, both bodies were replaced, and then additional bodies were interred atop theirs, like afterlife roommates. Headstones for the more recently deceased were installed to mark their resting place, but there's nothing to commemorate the Rathbones. It's a bit of historical irony almost too on the nose to be believable.

Another potentially unbelievable epilogue to the tragedy of Henry and Clara Rathbone follows the tainted dress Clara wore to the theatre that night. Though ruined after being soaked in Henry's blood, Clara couldn't bring herself to dispose of it. Instead, she stored it in a closet at her family's summer home in Albany. On April 14, 1866, one year to the day after the assassination, Clara, sleeping in the room where the dress was stored, suddenly awoke in the middle of the night to the vivid sound of low, familiar laughter. She concluded it was a ghostly echo of Abraham Lincoln's final moments, enjoying the comic performances of *Our American Cousin* just before the shot was fired.

Exactly one year later, a family guest sleeping in the same room came to breakfast with the same story. Clara concluded that the spectral sounds were connected to the presence of the dress. Still unwilling to destroy or part with the dress, Clara had the closet sealed off by installing a brick wall—in essence creating a tomb for the haunted dress. But even this didn't stop the ghostly occurrences.

For years afterward, residents of the house would hear a loud, single gunshot on the anniversary. Some saw the ghost of Abraham Lincoln, others the ghost of a young woman in a blood-smeared dress, crying. These stories circulated for decades, and well-known author Mary Raymond Shipman Andrews eventually captured a version of this gothic tale in a 1929 book called *The White Satin Dress.*

Finally, in 1910, just before Henry Rathbone died in Germany, his oldest son had the brick wall in the closet of the Albany house torn down, then removed the dress and burned it, saying it had cursed his family for nearly a half-century. While the dress itself may not have been the source of the misery, it certainly symbolized that which was—something beautiful tainted by blood. And two lives ultimately destroyed.

It's possible that Henry Rathbone's mental and emotional issues may well have surfaced even if he hadn't accompanied the Lincolns to the theatre that night. But it's difficult to not connect his eventual breakdown with the assassination. "He was never thoroughly himself after that night," his doctor explained to reporters after Clara's murder. "I have no hesitation in affirming that the dreaded tragedy, which preyed upon his nervous and impressionable temperament for many years, laid the seeds of that homicidal mania."

Often little more than a footnote to history, Henry Rathbone and Clara Harris provide an additional undercurrent of tragedy. Whether they endure as actual apparitions, they, the dress, and the subsequent domestic homicide linked to it hover over the Lincoln assassination like a dark spectral cloud—not unlike John Connally's vividly realistic nightmares or Nellie Connally's sudden shock of white hair.

When you look at both assassinations, it's not difficult to see ghosts, both figuratively and literally. Accompanying its respective phantoms, each assassination also contains its own haunted house—a pair of locations that endure to this day, steeped in tragedy, mystery, and an unquenchable fascination.

7

An Abandoned Church, a Tractor Store, and the Sorrows of Post-Assassination Resale Value

"It was a house without kindness," Shirley Jackson wrote in *The Haunting of Hill House*, "never meant to be lived in, not a fit place for people or for love or for hope. Exorcism cannot alter the countenance of a house; Hill House would stay as it was until it was destroyed."

Hill House was her greatest and most memorable literary creation. With her 1959 novel now the subject of two film adaptations and an extremely loosely based Netflix original series, it's endured as the template for all haunted house tales that have come since and the comparison point for any that came before. Her ability to turn a pile of bricks and mortar into a metaphorical character of such delicious gothic foreboding defines an entire genre of campfire stories, each built on the cornerstone that some buildings are simply born bad.

This is not to say that literal ghosts float through the hallways of Ford's Theatre and what was once known as the Texas School Book Depository. But it would be naive to state that either structure no longer carries with it some of the dark karma from the ghoulish event that defined each one. Nor should we posit the theory that there was something inherent in the construction or architectural DNA of each building—being built on unholy or cursed ground, for instance—that led to its ill repute.

That being said, the slightly sinister gravitas of each structure is undeniable. As you stand before and look upon them, they do seem to look right back. Not necessarily with malicious intent, but certainly with an undeniable power and perhaps a smidge of self-awareness. Not unlike Hill House, they stare at you with their eyes of blank windows beneath brows of brick cornice. Gazing at them, you get the feeling that, as Jackson describes in one of the great couplets of American literature, whatever walks there walks alone.

Of course, today nothing walks alone at either of these historic sites. A combined total of roughly a million people visit them each year, as they've both been transformed into tasteful and yet still powerful museums that explain these assassinations without glorifying or exploiting them.

"There is an element of pilgrimage," says David Byers, Supervisory Park Ranger at the Ford's Theatre National Historic Site, in an apt description that applies to both locations. "It's a place where you can connect with this story. I think people bring with them the sense of the power of the place. And once you get inside, there's a kind of tingle of anticipation and excitement."

But happily ever after and National Historic Places plaques didn't come easily for these infamous backdrops. Destruction, whether by the hand of fate or man, hovered like a cloud over both for decades after each assassination. There were long periods when the vision of flipping either one into a beautifully designed tourist attraction seemed about as likely as opening up a yoga studio on Venus.

These were roughly about the same odds of either of these places becoming tentpoles of history in the first place. Ordinary as ordinary can possibly get, each started out as something else altogether before taking on the role it would play in the death of a president. Curiously, each was also completely demolished early in its life cycle, only to be brought back to life by plucky entrepreneurs who, one could argue, may have been diverting a preemptive move by destiny to prevent epic catastrophe.

More likely, as we explored with Major Rathbone and Governor Connally, there's simply no way to sidestep history. Just as Rathbone and Connally are remembered for nothing more than being in the wrong place at the wrong time, equally fascinating stories surround these accidentally famous structures. Both of which suffered simply from *being* the wrong place at the wrong time.

Ford's Theatre, shown here draped in black crepe and guarded by soldiers immediately after the assassination, was reimagined and rebuilt several times over its often tragic history (Library of Congress).

If you're looking for an ethereal cause-and-effect explanation for tempting fate to turn against a piece of property, Ford's Theatre is the pony to bet on. Though the rationale is notably parochial.

It was built in 1834, 31 years before the assassination, not as a theatre but as a place of worship. The First Baptist Church held services there for much of the next three decades, led by eventual George Washington University founder Obadiah Brown, who served as pastor over a surprisingly diverse congregation. Middle and lower class, white and black parishioners worshiped together on the spot where the American patriarch of civil rights would eventually be slain. In 1859, First Baptist merged with another church and shifted its location to a larger and newer facility on Thirteenth Street.

The old church was put up for sale. After a Presbyterian church used it for a couple of years while its new location was being built, it began to be rented out for theatrical performances. Which wasn't unusual at the time and makes sense when you think about it: the structural similarity between a typical church and a theatre—a raised stage with semicircular seating arranged around it—lent the structure a new purpose. While common, the practice was still frowned upon by many. While every large city in the mid-nineteenth century had its share of theatres, they were still not fully embraced by the general populace as a respectable way to spend your evening—more akin to how some feel about casinos today.

So turning a house of God into "a devil's playhouse," as some critics referred to theatres, was enough for some to later conclude that the tragedy (plural tragedies, in fact) that would later unfold there was a result of this unholy transition.

In other words, the joint was cursed.

John Ford certainly didn't believe in that. The oldest of a trio of brothers in the theatre business, Ford signed a 10-year lease for the old First Baptist Church in 1861, with the right to purchase it for $10,000. Ford had successfully opened theatres in other cities and wanted to test the waters in the nation's capital before planting roots. While the enterprise was his initiative, he was, in fact, only loosely involved once it was up and running. His brothers Harry and James were the ones who managed the day-to-day operation and would become significant historical characters because of it.

Ford started his new Washington theatre with a series of minstrel shows, then embarked on the first of what would be several remodeling projects in the building's history, adding over 1000 seats. When the theatre re-opened in March of 1862, it was renamed Ford's Atheneum (which, thankfully for all the writers who would need to spell out the name of the building countless times over the years, didn't last). With the upgrade and name change, Ford was attempting to attract a more elite demographic. The performance docket reflected this, primarily focusing on witty comedies and Shakespearean plays. Ford's strategy worked, demonstrated by Abraham Lincoln making the first of what would be nine visits to the theatre on May 28, 1862, for a musical concert. Of course, those who were repulsed by the idea of a God-fearing individual spending an evening at the theatre criticized the president for doing such. "Some think I do wrong to go to the opera and the theatre, but it rests me," Lincoln once said in retort. "I love to be alone, and yet to be with the people." Thus, with the president providing an unspoken and unsolicited stamp of approval, Ford appeared to have successfully expanded his theatrical empire to the nation's capital.

Seven months later, it all seemed to come crashing down. Just after sunset on December 30, a faulty gas meter under the stage caused a fire to break out. Though no one was killed and the fire was put out before it could turn the entire building to ash, the damage was severe. Ford could have dropped his investment and moved on, but instead he doubled down. Gathering $75,000 from investors, he exercised the right to buy the theatre, along with two adjoining lots for expansion. He envisioned and designed a completely new theatre—similar to the look and feel of his Holliday Street Theatre in Baltimore—and less than two months after the original structure had been nearly obliterated, construction on the new version began. In August, just six months later, it reopened (now known as "Ford's New Theatre") better and busier than ever. It would be the site of nearly 500 performances over the next 20 months before going on a century-long hiatus.

That fall, Abraham Lincoln attended a pair of performances at the theatre within a two-week period, and would make three more trips to Ford's in December. The most memorable of the quintet of visits, both for him and for history, occurred on November 9—ten days before he recited the Gettysburg Address. That night he saw *The Marble Heart*, a fantastic tale about a Greek sculptor whose marble creations come to life. Playing the role of the sculptor that evening for the president's pleasure was the man who would eventually kill him: John Wilkes Booth.

Let's sit with that for a moment: the president watched his eventual assassin in the same theatre where the assassin would shoot him. Perhaps even sitting in the exact same spot where he would be shot. In fact, it's this detail that serves as the hinge for the believability of the skin-crawling little story that follows.

Lincoln was accompanied by a handful of guests that evening, including his sister-in-law Emilie Helm's niece would later recount the story from her aunt's recollections that at three different times during the play, Booth muttered threats that were part of the script, but he would glare directly at Lincoln as he said them. On the third occasion, he even moved extreme stage left and pointed his finger right at the president. "Mr. Lincoln," Emilie whispered, "he looks as if he meant that for you." Lincoln, after considering the comment, is to have replied, "Well, he does look pretty sharp at me, doesn't he?"

An additional detail that Helm's niece includes in the tale is that the group was sitting in a lower box just beneath the presidential box, right at eye level with the actors on stage. So when Booth wagged his history-changing finger at Lincoln, he was mere inches away from him. The assassin and his eventual target, nose-to-nose, as if on a movie poster.

The problem is that there's no evidence that Lincoln ever sat anywhere but the presidential box when he attended Ford's Theatre. It's possible that on this one occasion the president and his guests may have been seated elsewhere, literally setting the stage for the incident, but we'll never know for sure one way or the other.

An addendum to the story, the veracity of which is also questionable, has Lincoln being so impressed with Booth's performance that he invited him to the White House as his guest (or, in version 1b of this same subplot, that Lincoln requested to meet with Booth backstage after the show). Needless to say, Booth declined the potential invitation, however it was hypothetically offered.

Skeptical though the epilogue to the story may be, Lincoln seeing Booth in *The Marble Heart* at Ford's Theatre that night is proven fact. It's the Lincoln assassination equivalent of Lee Harvey Oswald writing a letter to John Connally a few months before shooting him, but even creepier. Not unlike the fate of the theatre, and many of its employees, after the assassination.

With everything about theatre culture already viewed with some skepticism by moralists, many leapt to the worst conclusions once word spread that the president had been assassinated in a theatre. Mary Lincoln herself expressed this disdain as she was escorted from the Petersen House after her husband had died. She glanced

THE ASSASSINATION OF PRESIDENT LINCOLN.
AT FORD'S THEATRE WASHINGTON.D.C.APRIL 14TH 1865.

A depiction of the tragic moment in the presidential box at Ford's Theatre (Library of Congress).

across Tenth Street at Ford's Theatre and sighed, "Oh, that dreadful house."

The immediate line of thought by investigators, unjustified as it turned out to be, was that it could have been an inside job. An actor had committed a murder in a theatre during a play that included many other actors he was acquainted with. And it was a theatre and a play he knew well, having performed in it himself at least 14 times. Consequently, he was able to perfectly time the shot he fired for the longest and loudest laugh of the show.

Guards were immediately posted at all entrances to the theatre, and many actors and employees were taken into custody, including all three Ford brothers, who were held for questioning for several weeks. Even after he was released, it would be months before John Ford—who wasn't even in Washington that night—regained access to his own theatre. There had been some discussion throughout the early summer that the YMCA might purchase the theatre and turn it into a combination Christian reading room/lecture hall, while keeping the presidential box in tact as a shrine to Lincoln. A fundraising effort was put in motion, but quickly fell apart. Once it did, Ford decided to plow full steam ahead and reopen the theatre in the hope that the tragedy—or at least his theatre's part in it—would soon be forgotten. Little did he know that was never going to happen.

In an unintentional bit of symbolism, Ford regained control of the theatre on the same day that Booth's conspirators were executed. His plan was to reopen on July 10 with the same performance that had originally been scheduled for April 15. Tickets sold briskly, and it appeared that Ford would indeed be able to return to business as usual. Then, on July 9, Ford received an anonymous letter.

> *Sir: You must not think of opening tomorrow night. I can assure you that it will not be tolerated. You must dispose of the property in some other way ... build another and you will be generously supported. But do not attempt to open it again.*
>
> —*One of many determined to prevent it*

With this not-so-veiled threat combined with vague rumors swirling that the theatre would be burned to the ground or angry mobs would swarm it if business were to resume, Secretary of War Edwin Stanton once again took over the building and shut it down.

"It's sort of unknown what the level of outrage is," Byers says. "There's certainly the story that the people wouldn't have it and they threatened to burn the theatre down. John Ford would insist that was not the case, that that's not what was in the air. Edwin Stanton felt differently, although it's hard to know if Stanton was just reacting out of his own personal revulsion at the idea, or if he's really responding to what he sees as a threat to public safety."

Ford was furious, placing a sign on the door reading "Closed by order of the Secretary of War"—making it clear to his disappointed customers that Stanton was responsible for their spoiled evening. Feeling robbed, Ford filed a lawsuit demanding compensation from the government. In a rare moment of self-awareness for a raw deal it was imposing on one of its citizens, the government agreed to lease the building from Ford for $1,500 a month with an option to purchase. It was basically the same deal Ford had struck with the First

Baptist Church when he first acquired it. A year later, the government bought the building from Ford for $88,000.

The decision was made to turn it into an office building, and the entire structure was gutted, wiping out all of the reconstruction work Ford had overseen just three years earlier. But amid the destruction, a fascinating mystery emerges.

In August, newspaper accounts describe the beginning of dismantling, noting that while the stage and other elements had been removed, the presidential box remained in place. A week later, further accounts now noted that the box and related pieces had been removed and were being kept safely under lock and key. In the years to come, this was proven to be at least partially true when articles of furniture from the box and the actual door to the box that Booth peered through before entering were donated by the descendants of the Ford family.

But parts of the box itself never emerged. It seems unlikely that the box—primarily the more noteworthy elements like the railing Booth leapt from—would have been casually tossed aside or forgotten, or that the newspaper accounts of the time that mentioned the elements of the box being saved would be incorrect. Or, for that matter, that Ford, who was a savvy businessman, would not have seen the intrinsic (and potentially lucrative) value in the box itself as he had with the other pieces. "The rest of the elements of the box clearly existed and were removed and put away," Byers says, "but they have not come to light."

Which begs two questions: what happened to these pieces, and are they still out there somewhere? Could the actual presidential box Lincoln was shot in be sitting in a garage or attic somewhere, perhaps even unbeknownst to the owner, waiting for someone to make a wonderful discovery?

Once the presidential box and (so everyone hoped) all the corresponding bad memories had been stripped, the building became functional again. Initially, Stanton thought there would be poetic symbolism in using the tainted structure to store the Confederate government's war records. Eventually, it was used for the Office of Records and Pensions, where veterans' pension requests would be processed and stored on the first two floors. The third floor became the home of the Army Medical Museum, which, even outside of its dubious location, was a bizarre little endeavor. It displayed surgical tools alongside random body parts and skeletons, primarily as examples of Civil War medical treatments. It would have been weird anywhere, but made all the more maudlin being housed in Ford's Theatre, even though the museum had no intentional connection to the building's history.

Well, almost no connection. Curiously, one of the items on display in the museum was part of John Wilkes Booth's spine. His name wasn't listed on the corresponding description, just the date of his death. Still, it makes you wonder how "the many determined to prevent" Ford's Theatre from opening out of respect to the president would have felt about this. Or, for that matter, the next notable event for the building—which was still a little ways off.

The shared office/museum space remained in operation over the next several decades. During this period, America's second presidential assassination took place, just eight tenths of a mile from Ford's Theatre, when James Garfield was shot by Charles Guiteau in the Baltimore and Potomac Railroad Terminal at Sixth Street and Constitution Avenue. On the historical marker that was placed at the spot of the shooting in 2018 near what is now the National Gallery of Art's West Building, Ford's Theatre is marked on the artistically incorporated map to help provide a sense of geography. And perhaps subtly underline the unnerving geographic proximity between the spots.

The Medical Museum eventually moved out and the Office of Records and Pensions absorbed the entire building, housing 500 clerks at its peak. The office remained open during an 1893 construction project that dug twelve feet into the basement floor. On a Friday morning that June, a supporting pier in the construction area gave way and all three floors of the building collapsed. Sixty-five people were injured and 22 were killed. "Hundreds of men carried down by the floors of a falling building which was notoriously insecure," the *Indianapolis Journal* breathlessly described in an over-the-top, yet not uncommon, snapshot of nineteenth-century journalism. "Human lives crushed out by tons of brick and iron and sent unheralded to the throne of their Maker; men by the score maimed and disfigured for life; happy families hurled into the depths of despair."

Now having endured its second tragedy (third if you count the fire of 1862), whispers swirled through the capital that the building was indeed cursed, most likely because of the original sin of transforming it from a church to a theatre.

An even creepier little coincidence dovetails with this story. On the same morning that Ford's Theatre collapsed, John Wilkes Booth's brother Edwin, an equally famous actor overshadowed by his brother's actions, was laid to rest in Cambridge, Massachusetts, after dying two days before. Once again, write it off if you will, but the symbolism is there. It was as if both Edwin's life and death were tainted by tragic events within Ford's Theatre.

Whether or not there were emotional scars in Ford's Theatre, there certainly were physical ones. Even after the damage was cleared and repaired, the building was deemed structurally unsound enough to support workers as it had before, and was shifted solely for use as a warehouse for storage. An economy and efficiency commission organized by President William Howard Taft attempted to condemn the building in 1912, but, as it had for nearly a century, Ford's Theatre endured.

Coinciding with the fiftieth anniversary of the assassination, new interest in the event and an appreciation for the building began to take root. In 1924, a plaque was mounted outside Ford's Theatre, officially identifying it as the place where Lincoln was shot. On hand at the unveiling was Illinois congressman Henry Rathbone—the son of the other victim of the assassination, who'd grown up with relatives after the death of his mother and his father's incarceration. The junior Rathbone would pass away four years later, but not before introducing legislation to fund a renovation of Ford's Theatre to turn it into a Lincoln museum. His proposal ultimately failed to garner support, but kept the torch burning to light the way toward a greater vision.

With the transfer of control of the building that same year from the War Department to the Office of Public Buildings & Public

Parks of the National Capital, the stage was set for change. Just as Henry Rathbone's offspring played a role in the rescue of Ford's Theatre, so too did Ulysses S. Grant III, grandson of the former general and president. Grant III was the Director of Public Buildings, and found money in his budget to open up a Lincoln museum in the theatre in 1932. It garnered little attention at first, but attendance gradually picked up over the years, as did its collection of artifacts. The derringer pistol Booth used to shoot Lincoln, for example, was acquired from the Judge Advocate General's office in 1940, followed in 1959 by the couch Rathbone was sitting on and the portrait of George Washington that hung outside the box—both donated by John Ford's great grandson. A detailed miniature diorama of the theatre drew attention, as did a mostly creepy recreation of the presidential box using wax figures. Still, the entire enterprise somehow felt out of place, even in such an historic and directly connected location. The museum looked and felt like a bus station, since there was no real effort to connect the assassination to the building it took place in.

Over the next several decades, the long, arduous process toward renovation began. And in another twist, John Kennedy played a big part in it. As he rode in his inaugural parade in January 1961, he was struck by what rough shape much of downtown Washington was in. He kickstarted a plan to help enliven the area, which paralleled nicely with the campaign to bring Ford's Theatre back to life. Even more ironically, Kennedy's assassination rejuvenated interest in Lincoln's murder, and support for restoring Ford's Theatre grew even stronger. On July 7, 1964 (99 years to the day since Booth's conspirators were put to death in yet another coincidental quirk), Congress appropriated $2 million in reconstruction costs. Work began in 1965 to refurbish the theatre to its appearance of 100 years earlier, including building the facade of the Star Saloon next door and a Lincoln museum in the basement.

Work was completed in late 1967, with the original idea to use the refurbished theatre for nothing more than tours and light-show lectures telling the story of what happened there. Eventually the decision was made that once again putting on shows there would celebrate Lincoln and his love for the theatre. It would also, the argument went, help prevent most people's fear that the theatre would turn into a shrine to Booth and his deeds.

On January 30, 1968, Ford's Theatre was the site of a performance for the first time in over a century. In a nationally televised broadcast, stage actress Helen Hayes opened things up by walking onto the stage and reciting a portion of *Our American Cousin* as the empty presidential box was illuminated by lights. It opened a gala performance that included appearances by stars like Harry Belafonte, Andy Williams, and Henry Fonda. While the Sunday-night event came off beautifully, it seemed Ford's Theatre still couldn't escape another hip check from history. As the show unfolded in Washington, on the other side of the globe, the Tet Offensive began, steering the U.S. into its darkest period of the Vietnam War.

Thus, Ford's Theatre was finally reborn, carrying on through the remainder of the century and into the next as both an historical site and a throwback theatre. In April 1975, Gerald Ford became the first president since Lincoln to visit Ford's when he attended the theatre's annual gala, which remains a huge event in the capital, often broadcast on national television. (Five months later, Ford became the first president to be nearly assassinated twice in a three-week period. Read into that what you will.)

Neither Ford nor any other chief executive or guests have watched a performance from the rebuilt presidential box, which remains closed off. During tours, guests can step up to the doorway and peer in to visualize what happened there. Which prompts some to wonder as they lean forward and crane their necks as far as they can into the forbidden area: did anything *really* happen there?

In a cosmic sense, of course the answer is yes. In terms of longitude and latitude that's unquestionably the spot where the assassination took place. But did it happen *there*? With careful, historical precision, both the theatre and the box were rebuilt to look exactly the way they did on the night Lincoln was shot. Or as close as possible. One notable (if not noticeable) difference is the height of the presidential box. Today it's roughly twelve feet above the stage, whereas in 1865 it was nine feet, making Booth's leap appear about 33 percent more impressive than it actually was.

Re-creation or not, it absolutely works. As you step into Ford's Theatre and make your way up the winding staircase and along the dress circle just as Booth did at 10 p.m. on that Good Friday, you truly do feel as if you're stepping back in time.

Though that feeling is less pervasive outside the theatre. The building itself is eye catching because of its clearly out-of-date appearance, but it's everything around it that truly draws your attention. If you take a stroll down Tenth Street today, Ford's Theatre and its environs look much more like an upscale shopping mall or sports arena. You'll see illuminated signage and light pole banners alongside souvenir stands selling Lincoln t-shirts, keychains, and action figures. More than ever, Ford's Theatre is impossible to miss. Which isn't a criticism. If anything, it's a perverse nod to just how far it's come: from church to theatre to office to disaster site to warehouse to museum back to theatre.

Now it's a tantalizing tourist destination, both the theatre itself and the museum in the basement, which has evolved over the years to focus more on the assassination. Its collection has grown to reflect this shift as well. For as much as the recreated theatre is the centerpiece of the site, the real power of the experience lies here in the basement. You stand before glass cases with the *actual* clothes Lincoln wore that night. With the *actual* contents of Booth's pockets when he was captured. With the *actual* gun he used to shoot Lincoln. "It seems surreal," Byers says. "You look at these things and wonder, 'How could this be that item, and how could it be *right here?*'"

The museum underwent extensive overhauls in 1988 and 2009 and is now a highly engaging and fascinating journey through the assassination. It's the perfect place to while away a muggy summer afternoon in the capital—a far cry from its days of sterile bus station ambiance.

But much like the Kennedy limousine that's eternally parked in a corridor at the Henry Ford Museum in Michigan, as you wander through the building, you have to ask yourself a broader version of the question you ask while peering into the box: is the Ford's Theatre that 650,000 visitors walk through every year the same Ford's The-atre that Lincoln was murdered in?

At this point, it's more of a philosophical question. "I kind of have to remind myself this is all recreated," Byers says. "It feels like a powerfully real place, even though it's not. Just to be that close to that element of history is a raw, powerful experience."

What little that remains of the original building is primarily along the brick front facade outside, with its arched doorways and window bays. Portions of the north and south walls are still origi-nal as well as some of the brickwork in the back alley and atop the roof.

Perhaps the more appropriate question is whether the limited authenticity takes away any of the historical significance of the site. And whether that has any effect on a visitor's experience.

"The overwhelming majority of people that visit have no idea that it's recreated," Byers admits. "They're thinking what they're see-ing is original. Which puts us in a little bit of an awkward position. I don't want to ruin the illusion and the mystique, and ultimately we're here to connect people to the story of the place. I don't want to get in the way of that just to make sure you know this is a recreation. But I don't want people leaving feeling like we didn't inform them or that they were robbed. Most people think that's original and I think that's fine."

These questions over what's original and what's not, as well as the authenticity of the visitors' experience, are less complicated at the theatre's doppelgänger deep in the heart of Texas.

***

One of the more fascinating—amusing, really, if you're comfort-able with that word in this context—aspects of the Kennedy assassi-nation is that many parts of it feel like a commercial.

In footage and photographs from that day, it's impossible not to notice corporate emblems virtually every step of the way. The East-ern Airlines logo on the stairs of the jetway visible as the Kennedys debark from Air Force One. A Dr. Pepper banner on the side of a city bus the motorcade passes. Quick glimpses along the parade route of a Ramada Inn, a Florsheim Shoes, a Neiman Marcus department store, and a Walgreen's Drugs.

Even if not visual, product placement oozes into the police reports and investigations that sift through the aftermath. Immediately after shooting Kennedy, Lee Harvey Oswald stops in the second-floor lunchroom to buy a Coca-Cola. Immediately before shooting Oswald, Jack Ruby stops by a Western Union office to send a telegram.

Of course, it all makes sense. These were snapshots from modern, post–World War II America, which, just as today, was littered with commercial product reminders in a consumer-based culture. We become so used to them in our day-to-day lives that they don't become truly noticeable until we see them in another context, like an examination of a massively historic event. Because of the endurance of many of these companies and products, these callouts remain recognizable today, making the assassination seem more real and less distant. In fact, after a while, seeing these familiar products we still use today alongside the characters and events of such an important moment in history starts to feel very surreal. You can almost hear a deep baritone voice announcing, "*The Kennedy Assassination is brought to you by....*"

Of all the elements of embedded marketing sprinkled throughout, there's one that stands above the rest. Quite literally, in fact, since the epicenter of the assassination was and always will be identified and associated with a billboard on its roof.

Overlooking Dealey Plaza, the Texas School Book Depository never had and never will have any architectural flair to it. The first time you look at it, you feel like you've seen it a million times. It's a square box of bricks that could be picked up and put down anywhere in the world and you wouldn't give it a second glance. What defined the building's visual identity, at least at the moment of its infamy, was a 23-foot long sign mounted atop the building that highlighted the merits of Hertz Rent a Car to the thousands of Dallas motorists who would see it each day.

It also included a large digital readout on its right side which would alternately flash the time and temperature. This was a fairly

The Texas School Book Depository (top center) overlooking Dealey Plaza—a surprisingly small patch of land which became the site of arguably the most memorable single moment in American history (Library of Congress).

novel technological breakthrough in the early '60s designed to draw the eye and one of just three such Hertz signs in the U.S. with the feature. Consequently, the billboard served as an asterisk to the building that marked the exact spot at which history changed forever. Such a reputation never would have been expected of the Texas School Book Depository, which had only been known by that name for a few months in 1963, but it would be cemented as its identity forever after.

Before we get to the origin story of Oswald's place of employment, we must set the stage by getting to know Dealey Plaza itself, which basically looks the same today as it did on that sunshiny November afternoon. The first thing that strikes you when you walk into the heart of the plaza is just how intimate and cozy it really is, closer in size and scope to a dog park. "It looks sweeping on television and in movies, but it's a remarkably small space," says Stephen Fagin, Curator of the Sixth Floor Museum at Dealey Plaza located inside the former Depository. "It's a truly unique site, and I don't think there can be a true appreciation of it until you stand there on Elm Street and take a look around."

What you'll see when you take a look around certainly wouldn't qualify as disrespectful, but on any given day, there is a little bit of a flea market flavor. The heavy and constant traffic sets the tone—cars zooming by on their way to the freeway, thinking about their commute or changing the radio station rather than the global significance of the road they're driving on. Conspiracy theorists set up tables on and near the infamous grassy knoll hawking their wares. Visitors march up and down the knoll and climb behind the picket fence atop it as if the answer to the mystery is still hidden there waiting to be discovered. Kids wait for breaks in traffic to race out onto Elm Street to take selfies with the Depository in the background—posing precisely on a large white X painted on the street to mark the exact spot where the fatal shot hit Kennedy.

For some (mostly older visitors), it's a place of extreme reverence and reflection. For others (mostly younger visitors), it is, as Fagin puts it, a giant real-life episode of *CSI*, where they try to solve a puzzle, almost akin to an historical escape room. "Dealey Plaza can be many things to many people," he says. "And whatever people bring to the site is what they take away."

Before it became the site of tragedy, Dealey Plaza was a triumph of architecture and engineering, garnering the reputation as the "front door of Dallas." John Nealy Bryan, the founder of the city, built a cabin on this spot of land overlooking the Trinity River in 1841—a replica of that cabin has stood along Elm Street close to the Depository since the 1930s. Evolving from a collection of wagon yards and livery stables in the late nineteenth century, the area that would become Dealey Plaza initially transformed into a warehouse district, primarily for farming-related companies.

At its heart, the plaza itself, beautiful as it would become, was created solely as a traffic solution. The triple underpass which defines it merges together three busy roads, winds them beneath elevated railroad tracks, and steers them toward freeway exits leading out of the downtown area. A massive undertaking built with Works Progress Administration funds in the middle of the Great Depression, the triple underpass and connecting plaza opened in the spring of 1936. Later beautification improvements turned it into a park-like spot, with concrete colonnades, stone pergolas, Art Deco shelters, reflecting pools (more commonly called "lagoons" by locals), and lush landscaping. It was named for George Bannerman Dealey, the publisher of the *Dallas Morning News* and a city figure who was instrumental in getting the project completed. He died shortly after its opening, so Dealey Plaza was actually a memorial long before it became a memorial.

Off to the side, the Depository building watched the area being torn down and rebuilt around it. Nearly as old as Dallas itself, the original version of the structure was built in 1899. Headquartered in Lincoln's home state of Illinois, the Rock Island Plow Company needed a warehouse and showroom to sell large agricultural equipment to farmers in the region. And like Ford's Theatre, it was smote down by calamity almost immediately. In May 1901, just two years after being built, the building was struck by lightning and burned to the ground. But also like Ford's, it was quickly rebuilt—now seven stories instead of the original five—and by November the structure that still stands there today was open for business.

The type of business conducted there would change quite a bit over the years. It remained an equipment warehouse and display area for decades as the farming industry burgeoned in the southwest in the early twentieth century. In the 1930s, the tractors and implements moved out and the building became the home of a company which manufactured and sold a novel new invention that would soon make Texas a bearable place to live: the air conditioner. A few years after that, it became a distribution center for the wholesale grocery company John Sexton & Co. and became known informally as the Sexton Building for the next two decades. In fact, in several of the initial police communications and reports on the day of the assassination, the Depository was referred to as the Sexton Building.

As the tenants came and went, the only thing that really defined the building through much of the post-war years was the variety of commercial signage that adorned its roof. It certainly was a prime location for such advertisements, with steady downtown traffic just beneath and a constant stream of cars coming into Dallas from Fort Worth passing by on the Stemmons Freeway just in front. Yet it was the only building in or around Dealey Plaza that wore a billboard like a Stetson. As it happened, it's pretty much the only building in Dealey Plaza that could have mounted commercial signage on its roof since the rest of the buildings along the square were all government operated. Still, it's almost as if destiny deemed that the Depository needed some sort of visual flair to identify it since it would soon become part of history.

The first sign was erected in 1942 just after the completion of Dealey Plaza, shilling U.S. Royal Tires. Replacing it in the 1950s was a large sign promoting Ford cars. Even for the agnostic, the thought of this sign being placed on a building that would soon become history's new version of Ford's Theatre is enough to provide a bit of a shiver.

In 1959, the Ford sign was replaced by the Hertz sign which would, unfortunately for Hertz, always be associated with the assassination. Of the series of billboards that adorned the building, it was the most impressive. While the digital clock and temperature readout on the right was the eye-luring hook, the Hertz logo itself was a snappy piece of work: red letters slaked back against a vibrant yellow background. And to the right, just beneath the digital clock, was the word "Chevrolets," as if to balance the commercial scales after a decade of the building promoting Ford. (Interestingly, a couple of years after the assassination, the "Chevrolets" addendum to the billboard was replaced by one reading "Fords.")

Much as it sounds like it should be, "Texas School Book Depository" wasn't the name of the building. It was the name of the company that leased the building—sort of like how "Frankenstein" wasn't actually the monster, but the man who created him. Founded in 1927, it was a privately owned firm that basically did exactly what its name suggested: it stored books that could be ordered by and shipped to various schools across the southwest, like a miniature Amazon.com. The company headquarters was still new to the neighborhood at the time of the assassination, moving the bulk of its operation into the vacant Sexton Building on Elm Street in early 1963.

Even with such an unfair blow to its name and reputation (with both an employee and its headquarters involved in the most heinous crime of the twentieth century), the Texas School Book Depository persevered after the assassination. But it wasn't easy. Starting on the weekend of the assassination, when the building was sealed off for investigation, it remained distinctly inhospitable. Going forward, its doors would be locked to the public, and employees required special access to come in and out of the building—commonplace in today's workplaces but highly unusual (and discomforting) in the 1960s. But there was a good reason for the precautions. Tourists were constantly trying to get inside, often attempting to bribe the employees to take them to the sixth floor for a look around. The company remained in the building for another seven years before relocating to a new facility in northwest Dallas. While business logistics certainly played into the decision, there was little doubt that the lasting echoes of the assassination were a big factor.

From that point, the Depository entered into the same lonely, seemingly hopeless post-assassination existence that Ford's Theatre muddled through. After the books were removed in 1970, the building was sold at auction for $650,000 to a music promoter and Kennedy memorabilia collector from Nashville named Aubrey Mayhew. Buying it more or less on impulse, Mayhew had a feverish vision of turning it into a Kennedy shrine and museum, like one he'd opened in Nashville. It didn't seem like a big deal at the time, but ultimately this was the key moment in the building's survival. "If anybody else had bid a dollar higher on that building," Fagin explains, "it would be a moot point. The building would have been torn down in 1970." Not that Mayhew really knew what he was doing. With no real plans of what he would build or how he would pay for it, the Depository remained vacant and essentially untouched for the next two years.

Even though little was happening with the Depository, by this point it had clearly become an albatross around the city of Dallas and a symbol of everything it wanted to forget. "There was this difficult process from loss to renewal," Fagin says, "as the community struggled to face down its demons and the stigma that for so many people was personified by the looming architecture of the School Book Depository."

Silly as it may sound to our more modern understanding of the senselessness of violence and tragedy, immediately after the assassination and for years after, many Americans actually blamed the city of Dallas for what had happened. Unfair as it was, there was some precedence. Even before the assassination, Dallas had earned the dubious nickname of the "City of Hate," primarily for some well-publicized political incidents involving right-wing nutjobs. Most memorably, United Nations Ambassador Adlai Stevenson being attacked by protestors after a speech a month before Kennedy visited Texas.

The assassination (even though it was performed by a *left*-wing nutjob) used up whatever tolerance the rest of the world had for the City of Hate. For instance, when the National Football League's Dallas Cowboys took the field in Cleveland for their first game following the assassination, they were vociferously booed by the home crowd, as if coach Tom Landry had driven Oswald's getaway car. Stories trickled back about Dallas residents traveling around the country and being ordered out of taxi cabs or having change thrown at them by gas station attendants. A Dallas-based Boy Scout troop visiting the World's Fair in New York in 1964 had to cover up any patches they were wearing that included the name of their city in the fear of getting beat up by fellow scouts.

Understandably, Dallas very much wanted to sweep any memories of the assassination under the rug and move on. And the idea of someone turning the nexus of Dallas's embarrassment into a shrine upset many residents and civic leaders. "A crumbling, condemned, ugly ... memorial to what?" a frustrated city councilman asked. "To the fanatic foul deed of a sick little man?"

Foul deeds continued to emerge from within the Depository. In July 1972, a mysterious fire caused serious damage to two floors of the vacant building and was determined to have been deliberately set. A caretaker was arrested and pled not guilty, claiming that Mayhew was actually behind the fire. Mayhew categorically denied it, and the caretaker received five years' probation. Still, some wondered if Mayhew had arranged it all as a last-gasp effort to bail himself out. The building was foreclosed upon ten days later and D. Harold Byrd, the oil tycoon who'd sold it to Mayhew two years before, bought it back at a nice profit. With the threat of turning the building into a museum now apparently snuffed out, the question remained of what to do with this taint on Dallas's ample pride.

A passionate movement was led to tear the building down. "If you erase the building, they can't photograph it," Fagin says. "I think it was just this naive idea that if we destroy the building, we can stop people from coming here and people will forget that this was the site of the assassination." Naive indeed, especially with Ford's Theatre having just been reborn as a nationally known tourist attraction and historic site—all while Dallas was rejecting the idea that the site of the Kennedy assassination was historically significant.

Yet even the Etch-a-Sketch solution for the Depository ran the risk of exploitation, as rumors swirled of speculators selling bricks from the demolished building for a dollar apiece. Gradually, as the tenth anniversary of the assassination came and went and an application to add the building to the National Register of Historic Places was denied, a low-grade, almost imperceptible understanding of the Depository's significance began to settle in. Even with nothing official there to commemorate the assassination, Dealey Plaza became the most popular tourist spot in Dallas, and was second only to the Alamo in all of Texas.

The mid–1970s were, much like the auction after the Texas School Book Depository moved out at the beginning of the decade, the most dangerous time for the building's survival. At any point, a wealthy, well-meaning Dallasite determined to clear the slate could have purchased the building and turned it to rubble. And perhaps with the Depository gone, the look and feel of Dealey Plaza would have been reimagined to further wipe the slate clean before the appreciation for history could take root.

Call it fate, call it destiny, but the uninhabited Depository remained in place for years, even with the drums of destruction beating around it. Eventually, the building found an unlikely champion. Public Works Director Judson Shook, who could see from his office window both the Depository and the constant stream of visitors taking pictures of it, became the Depository's unlikely savior. Successfully arguing that tearing the building down would make it look like Dallas was either hiding something or admitting its guilt, Shook introduced an acceptable compromise. Dallas County purchased the building in 1976 to use for office space, just like what had happened with Ford's Theatre a century earlier. This way the building could remain intact, but with the county owning it, there would be no fear of it being turned into a commercial emporium of bad taste.

Though, even in its utilitarian efforts, the county made sure the sixth floor remained unoccupied and undisturbed. Which, while done out of respect, only gave it more magnitude. "Your imagination could easily be carried away to thinking that the place was haunted," Shook said upon visiting the sixth floor for the first time. He noted in particular the power of the long and dark shadows that crept through the entire floor, which was already defined by exposed pipes along the walls and flickering light bulbs dangling from the ceiling.

Incredibly, through the assassination aftermath, the abandonment of the building, and the entire episode over what to do with it, the Hertz sign remained atop the Depository, easily identifying it to even the most novice of passersby as Dallas's House of Horrors. The sign—once referred to as "a tumorous growth" by a Texas senatorial candidate—remained on the roof for 16 years after the assassination. It was finally removed in 1979 because it was hurting the building. Symbolically, of course, since it was basically a scarlet letter for the entire city, but also quite literally. The weight of the sign was damaging the building's structural integrity, acting as a sail atop the roof and vibrating so much that it crumbled mortar out from between bricks on the top three floors. The Hertz company declined an offer to take the sign back, as did several other museums and historical societies. Included in that list was the Smithsonian, which saw no historical value in it (just as it had determined 100 years before with Lincoln's rocker). The sign was removed from the roof and the metal framework holding it up was discarded. But the museum kept the faceplate—the 128 pieces and parts that, when put together, actually reads "Hertz Rent a Car," along with the ceramic casings for the light bulbs and the

Symbolizing the frequency of commercial icons sprinkled throughout the narrative of the Kennedy assassination, the large Hertz sign mounted atop the roof of the Texas School Book Depository identified and defined the building for years (George Reid Collection/The Sixth Floor Museum at Dealey Plaza).

"Chevrolets" and "Fords" placards. The pieces remain hidden away in storage to this day, stuck in an historic catch-22: too big to put on display, too important to dispose of.

The removal of the Depository's halo of recognition marked the beginning of a new era for the building. With the assassination now nearing 20 years in the past, the embarrassment and stigma of it all finally began to fade. In its place came momentum for Dallas to finally accept and acknowledge the assassination and realize it had an obligation to history. Nothing reflected this more clearly than the effort to transform the Depository into a museum.

Whoops, wrong word.

"It was going to be a respectful, educational *exhibit*," Fagin points out. "Not a museum, an *exhibit*. A museum suggested permanence. When you think 'exhibition,' you think of it having a limited lifespan. They were so scared of the word 'museum' that they forbid its use in any of the content development or promotional material. They navigated that minefield very carefully."

Fundraising efforts began in the early 1980s, and organizers met with staff at Ford's Theatre (whom Fagin playfully calls "our American cousins") to get their thoughts and hear their stories. After progress was slowed by Ronald Reagan's near-assassination by John Hinckley (a Dallas native who'd researched the JFK assassination before attempting to impress Jodie Foster with his sociopathic nonsense), they picked up again as the 1980s marched on.

As did the Depository's tendency to burst into flames. Another arson attempt in the summer of 1984 (while the Republican National Convention was taking place at the Dallas Convention Center just a few blocks away) caused $250,000 in damage. Though this time no one was caught. Thus, fortune once again smiled on the Depository as it sidestepped potential destruction.

Through it all, the long journey toward commemoration continued. It eventually became reality in February of 1989 when the carefully named Sixth Floor Museum (the word by now no longer taboo) opened. And it was generally accepted right away, though attendance slagged a bit below expectations the first couple of years. After Oliver Stone's volcanic film *JFK* was released in 1991, attendance at the museum literally quadrupled and has remained steady ever since, integrating itself into the cultural fiber of Dallas. "Not bad for a building that a lot of people wanted to tear down," Fagin says with notable pride.

Not bad at all. True to its name, the museum is, for the most part, contained within the confines of the sixth floor, though it takes a solid hour and a half to make it through the array of displays and presentations, either on your own or by listening to an audio guide. It's expanded a bit over the years to include some exhibitions on the seventh floor and a research center on the first floor. The remainder of the building still contains Dallas County offices, so the original vision of the compromised rebirth of the Depository remains intact more than four decades later.

The narrative flow of the museum takes visitors through Kennedy's life and legacy before focusing on his trip to Dallas and the events of that November Friday. The museum offers educational programs and fantastic interactive elements on its website, including a 24/7 live web cam looking down from the Depository into the Plaza. Of course, the centerpiece of it all is the sniper's perch in the southeast corner of the sixth floor, which is very carefully conceived and preserved. Just like the box at Ford's Theatre, visitors can't enter Oswald's sniper's perch or gaze directly out the corner window, but they can step right up to a perimeter of plexiglass surrounding it to see exactly what it looked like at 12:30 p.m. on November 22, 1963.

Here perhaps is where the Depository most differs from Ford's Theatre. While the presidential box that's in the theatre today is actually just a very carefully designed recreation, the Depository's sniper's perch has remained relatively untouched and, consequently, almost exactly what it was in 1963. Several bricks were chiseled out of the wall along the left side of the perch by souvenir hunters and some restoration work was required, but for the most part, the wall still contains the original masonry. The boxes stacked around the sniper's nest are reproductions, but the floor they sit on contains the actual planks of wood that were there at the time. On the day of the assassination, plywood was being installed atop the planks of the sixth floor to protect the boxes of schoolbooks from an oily residue left over from the Sexton years. The job was finished soon after the assassination, and with the hesitancy to make any changes to the sixth floor, the plywood laid down that week remained in place for decades. When it was finally removed as the museum was built, it revealed the actual planks of wood that Lee Harvey Oswald stood upon when he fired his rifle.

The circular light fixtures hanging from the ceiling throughout the sixth floor have been rewired, but the exteriors are original. Even the actual window Oswald shot from has been on display at the museum. Or at least they think it was.

Like the Kennedy assassination itself, there are varying versions of the story that follows—pick the one you like. Option A has D. Harold Byrd, the building's owner in 1963, ordering the sniper's perch window removed from the building six weeks after the assassination and then displaying it in his home for the rest of his life. In 1994, a decade after his death, his son loaned the window to the museum, and it was on display near the sniper's nest recreation for the next twelve years. But from the moment it went on display, assassination researchers had doubts about its authenticity. Paint and putty smudges on the window didn't match the window's appearance in photographs from 1963, which has led to many questions.

An alternate version of the story claims that Byrd had the wrong window removed, and it was Aubrey Mayhew who actually took the correct one just before he gave up ownership of the building following his failed museum bid in 1972. Mayhew attempted to sell his window on eBay in 2007, albeit without providing any documentation proving why his was the right window and Byrd's was the wrong one. Byrd's son objected, not only claiming that he had the actual window (returned from the museum after being on display), but also offering *his* up for sale on eBay and suing Mayhew. Byrd's was purchased for a whopping $3 million (skyrocketing from its original $100,000 asking price) by a buyer from the Netherlands who, in a fitting end to the story, turned out to not actually have the money. As lawyers girded their loins for Window Wars, both principal parties died within a two-year period, and the legal proceedings sputtered out, leaving the question still officially unanswered. The museum takes no position on which window is the correct one. Even while Byrd's was on display, the corresponding language describing it was carefully constructed to make it clear that this was *a* window, not necessarily *the* window. All we know for sure is that the actual window was definitely removed at some point and that at least one of the two men was either mistaken or outright lying when he claimed provenance.

The confusion over the window oddly reflects the generations-long hand-wringing over what to do with the Depository itself. Today, the Sixth Floor Museum is not only a triumph of tightroping across the abyss of a controversial historical event, but stands as a physical manifestation of a city's catharsis. It's become the most visited tourist attraction in Dallas, with 400,000 visiting the museum each year. Similarly, after years of denials, Dealey Plaza was finally pronounced a National Historic Landmark District in 1993. The level

As ordinary-looking as a structure could be, the Texas School Book Depository became one of the most recognized buildings in the world (Library of Congress).

of respectability it had taken Ford's Theatre over 100 years to reach was achieved by the Depository in less than 30.

In the end, taking remarkably similar winding paths, both Ford's Theatre and the Texas School Book Depository somehow made it to the other side of historical infamy, and today are, if not exactly celebrated, certainly respected. Culturally we've accepted what's happened there and, in our fascination about these events and their impact, we seek these places out and include them as must-sees on family vacations.

Kind of like if Hill House were turned into a cozy bed and breakfast.

8

Assassination Goes
to the Movies

Whether we agree with it or not, the greatest indication of how culturally important an historic event is regarded generally tends to be reflected by Hollywood's acceptance, treatment, and repetition of it.

Take World War II, for example. As the most globally significant chapter of the twentieth century, it's continued to be a source of story material for the film industry for well over 75 years. And it makes perfect sense. Sifting through the nearly decade-long duration of the war, writers and historians can find countless tales of tragedy and triumph, adversity and survival taking place in trenches and towns back home. Many are completely fictional and many more are, in the parlance of Hollywood's favorite catchphrase, "based on a true story." The sheer volume of movies made from the genre keep that dark chapter alive in our cultural consciousness and, in the best cases, help us better understand and appreciate its significance.

But World War II—as well as the Civil War and Vietnam, two other prime examples—lasted for several years, playing out in hundreds of places and involved millions of people. More short-term historical events certainly get their day in Hollywood, but generally not enough to warrant their own genre.

The exception, not surprisingly, are the Lincoln and Kennedy assassinations, which, combined, have enough films dedicated to them to launch a streaming service. Thus, the sheer volume of motion pictures—and the similarities in their cadence and coverage—is yet another string tying these two events together that's worth exploring. That being said, for as much as there is to comment about the similarities, the differences between the film treatments of these two subjects might say even more.

Altogether, when you add up the films that either focus on the specific events or tell a broader story that includes a depiction of one of the two assassinations, you wind up with a total of well over 40 titles covering more than a century of filmmaking. Which is nothing short of astounding. And that's not even counting the hundreds of hours of documentary films that have been dedicated to these subjects—what follows is solely an examination of the scripted, "fictionalized" depictions.

Let's start by putting that number into context. Based largely on the success of and modeled after a handful of the Lincoln-Kennedy assassination films, the shooting of Ronald Reagan garnered a pair of made-for-TV movies. But pivoting to our control group, when we look into how many Hollywood films have depicted the assassinations of William McKinley or James Garfield, what do we find? A grand total of zero. So it's not merely a fascination with assassination that's drawing viewers to films of this sort, but fascination with *these* assassinations.

For what it's worth, a 1969 Spaghetti Western called *The Price of Power* does center around a fictional assassination attempt of President Garfield. Yet in essence, the entire piece is an unapologetic (and kind of hilarious) variation of the Kennedy assassination translated into cowboy times. Garfield is shot at in 1881 in the then-frontier town of Dallas, Texas, by a gunman high atop a cliff as the president is riding in an open-top stagecoach. So even when filmmakers hint at another assassination, they can't help but return to the one that sells tickets.

It's also worth noting that it was the shooting of William McKinley that inspired the first assassination-based film. One of the first films ever made, in fact—though using the term "film" quite liberally. In October 1901, roughly a month after McKinley's death, Thomas Edison's fledgling film studio produced a two-shot vignette, just over a minute long. A sad young woman representing Columbia, the female personification of America, sits at the base of a tomb (that looks much like what the Lincoln Memorial would become 20 years later). As she mourns, the faces of the then-three assassinated presidents appear at the top of the stairs. In the final seconds, the film cuts to a single assassin with crazed black hair, his back to the camera, lying prostrate at the foot of a statue of Lady Justice, presumably begging for forgiveness. Edison's studio would follow this up a month later with a three-minute reenactment not of McKinley's assassination, but of his assassin Leon Czolgosz's execution.

But these primitive one-reelers can hardly be considered movies by any modern standard. That trend began over the next decade, and not surprisingly, one of the first (and most infamous) full-length films ever made paid tribute to the Lincoln assassination.

Even at the time, D.W. Griffith's *Birth of a Nation* was considered controversial for its weapons-grade racism and highly revisionist take on post–Civil War Reconstruction. Released in 1915, marking the fiftieth anniversary of the end of the war, it was the first box office blockbuster. With an epic three-hour run time—truly remarkable for a silent film—it covers a wide range of time and topics, but primarily focuses on the causes of the war and its aftermath, with the Lincoln assassination serving as the breakpoint.

For the many, *many* fatal flaws of this film, this initial depiction of the president's murder is actually very accurately and efficiently crafted. The facsimile of Ford's Theatre looks just like (and in some cases is superior to) the dozens of others that would follow over the next century. While Booth is made out to look like a zombie roaming the corridors of the theatre, the staging and cinematography of the entire sequence are actually very admirably done.

Which is somewhat surprising, since Griffith didn't quite know what to do with Lincoln. Since the film leans hard into celebrating pre-war Southern culture (to the point that it seems to be trying to portray slavery as a quirky and fun endeavor for all involved), the president is clearly made out to be the villain and a reviled threat to the power of individual states. Yet it also correctly frames Lincoln's plan for post-war America as merciful, and the assassination as a dramatic turning point that spiraled Reconstruction into the mess it became. "When the terrible days were over and a healing time of peace was at hand ... came the fated night of April 14,

1865," reads one of the narrative slides leading into the assassination scene.

Griffith would take another shot at that night 15 years later in one of his final films. *Abraham Lincoln* is a straight biopic, telling the winding story of the president's life, and consequently, the assassination doesn't come up until the last 10 minutes. Staged essentially the same way as in *Birth of a Nation*, it's again fairly accurate, though Griffith does show Lincoln rising to speak and repeating bits from his second inaugural address from the presidential box as he arrives at Ford's. Which, of course, never happened.

But showing things that never happened is a part of the assassination movie genre. For instance, the initial film to cover the Kennedy killing was 1964's *The Trial of Lee Harvey Oswald*. From the title alone, we know this is a flight of fancy through an alternate reality. Yet it stays remarkably close to the vest. Filmed in Dallas just a few months after the assassination and released even before the Warren Commission Report was complete, it consists of a series of actors portraying real witnesses (with their names changed) in a faux courtroom drama imagining what due process would have looked like had Oswald lived. Indeed, a sour-faced actor was hired to be the first of a multitude to play Oswald over the years. He never speaks, just sits solemnly at the defense table as the camera zooms in for extreme close ups of his eyes darting around the courtroom, which leaves no doubt as to which way the verdict would go—though they do "leave it up to the viewer" to make up their own mind at the end.

It was an idea so nice, they made it twice. After adapting the same concept into a stage play in 1967, eventually the same title was used for a two-part TV miniseries that appeared on ABC in the fall of 1977. It features versatile character actor John Pleshette as Oswald and, in between runs on *Bonanza* and *Battlestar Galactica*, TV legend Lorne Greene as his fictional lawyer. This one does delve more into the "what if" of it all, imagining the alternate reality well into 1964, with Oswald's trial stretching out over six weeks. Along the way, it flashes back to the events of November 22 and then beyond, showing Oswald's travails in Russia. Though the series certainly doesn't sympathize with Oswald—eventually having him testify from a glass cage in the back of the courtroom as if he were Hannibal Lecter—it hedges its bet. It concludes with Jack Ruby shooting Oswald on his way to the courtroom before the verdict can be delivered.

"What if" exercises aside, the vast majority of assassination films are just-the-facts-ma'am depictions. They make up the final minutes of high-profile network mini-series: *Kennedy* with Martin Sheen in the title role in 1983 and its counterpart *Lincoln* with Sam Waterston in 1988, both on NBC. Then there's the equally balanced *Killing Lincoln* and *Killing Kennedy*, based on the Bill O'Reilly bestsellers and released just a few months apart in 2013 on the National Geographic Channel. *The Day Lincoln Was Shot* is another solid effort based on Jim Bishop's classic book that premiered on TNT in 1998 featuring Rob Morrow as a convincing John Wilkes Booth and Lance Henriksen as a doomed Lincoln.

The Kennedys, an embattled eight-part miniseries featuring Greg Kinnear as John Kennedy and Katie Holmes as Jackie, premiered in 2011 and deftly handles the assassination in its final two episodes—though quickly enough to also squeeze in Robert Kennedy's death 20 minutes later. A year later, Steven Spielberg took an even more oblique approach, deciding that he didn't need to depict the shooting of the president in his Oscar-winning *Lincoln*. Instead, he reveals the assassination from the point of view of young Tad Lincoln, who was attending another play across town that night. Spielberg does close the movie with the haunting scene in Lincoln's death room, where Daniel Day-Lewis takes his final breath in what will likely go down as the finest theatrical representation of the sixteenth president.

As it happens, Spielberg's portrayal of Tad's experience typified another angle of several films in this collection: showing the assassination and its impact from a real-life supporting character's point of view.

The Prisoner of Shark Island, released in 1936, was the first experiment of this kind and today stands as an interesting—if a bit strange—standalone side story. The focus of the tale is Dr. Samuel Mudd, the doctor who set Booth's broken leg after Booth had escaped to Maryland the night of the assassination. After a clumsily inaccurate portrayal of the assassination, the film leaves out the part that ultimately got Mudd in trouble. After having his leg repaired, Booth and companion David Herold simply depart Mudd's house rather than staying the night as they actually did. Therefore Mudd's choice to not turn in the pair the following day when he realized who they were—instead, instructing them to leave his farm—is not shown. In the film, Mudd is simply arrested, tried, and convicted solely for aiding a stranger in the middle of the night.

This omission makes the rest of the film much more powerful as a nightmarish tragedy. We see Mudd imprisoned at Fort Jefferson on the island of Dry Tortugas, Florida, which the movie breathlessly labels as "a bit of burning white hell," where "life imprisonment was an ironic term for slow death." After a dashing failed escape attempt, Mudd is redeemed when he steps up to help control an outbreak of yellow fever that swarms the prison. Consequently, Mudd is pardoned by President Andrew Johnson after four years, and he returns home to his family.

More accurate is *Prince of Players*, released 20 years later, in which legendary actor Richard Burton portrays legendary actor Edwin Booth. We see his rise to fame on the stage, followed by his budding rivalry with younger brother John Wilkes. Ultimately the film settles upon Edwin's adversity following the assassination, as once-adoring fans now turn on him and even blame him for the death of Lincoln at the hands of Edwin's brother.

The best and most heartbreaking of this collection on the Lincoln side of the fence is 2010's *The Conspirator*, which also centers on a victimized bystander. In the assassination's only real courtroom drama, director Robert Redford primarily focuses on the tragic story of Mary Surratt, played to tortured perfection by Robin Wright. Surratt, who owned the boarding house where Booth's plot was hatched but almost certainly had no knowledge of it, was ultimately sentenced to death with the rest of Booth's conspirators despite shoddy evidence, tainted testimony, and a more-than-questionable trial.

There are many more fertile supporting characters to explore within the Kennedy assassination. Naturally, Jackie Kennedy is an alluring draw, and became the centerpiece of the 1991 three-part miniseries *A Woman Named Jackie* and the 2016 feature film *Jackie*, starring Natalie Portman. While the miniseries includes the assassination as a brief subplot in a sprawling biographic profile, *Jackie* leverages the assassination and its immediate aftermath as its anchor. Portman earned an Oscar nomination for her portrayal of the First Lady in the deepest throes of depression, when she created the "Camelot" veneer brushed atop the Kennedy legacy.

The following year, *LBJ*, starring Woody Harrelson in heavy makeup, tries to follow the same template but doesn't manage it quite as gracefully. Focusing entirely on Johnson's transition to president over the assassination weekend, there are glimpses of the complicated man that Johnson was, but not enough for the film to stick the landing. Whereas *All the Way*, an HBO original movie based on a Broadway play released just a few months earlier and starring Bryan Cranston as LBJ, does much more with these ideas in less time, ultimately pivoting into the larger story of Johnson spearheading the Civil Rights Act into law.

Just barely qualifying as "based on a true story" is *An American Affair*, which centers on a quirky young woman in the aftermath of the assassination. Named Catherine Caswell in the film, the character was inspired by a young Georgetown artist named Mary Pinchot Meyer, who had a clandestine affair with the president (and, the movie suggests, may have been spying on him). The film follows her friendship with a creepy young boy who lives across the street and watches it all unfold. In the fateful days following the assassination, Caswell winds up dead at the bottom of the iconic *Exorcist* stairs (which didn't happen in reality) for reasons vaguely inferred but ultimately unexplained.

Whereas the Lincoln assassination movie catalog has several "victim" stories, the only one we get from the JFK portion is the 1993 TV movie *Fatal Deception: Mrs. Lee Harvey Oswald*. Featuring Helena Bonham Carter as Marina Oswald, we see a handful of refreshing, if painful, angles of her post-assassination reality: Marina seeking a place to live while carrying the burden of her husband's name, and her young daughters struggling with the awkward, unwanted attention that would follow the family long after Marina had moved on and remarried. Like some of the other Oswald-centric films, this one bounces back to Russia, where we see the couple meet, marry, and begin a family. As things turn dark in the marriage upon their return to America, the movie stays somewhat neutral by never quite showing what Oswald was up to, primarily focusing on Marina's largely shrouded point of view.

Interestingly, the majority of any and all JFK supporting-character stories are covered in a single film. *Parkland*, released just before the fiftieth anniversary in 2013, serves as the *Rosencrantz and Guildenstern Are Dead* to the assassination's *Hamlet.* It weaves together a fascinating smorgasbord of tales of what was happening in the less-visible pockets of the weekend of the assassination while the world's primary attention was pointed elsewhere. From the sweaty, bloody efforts of the overmatched medical staff at the titular Parkland Hospital to the thankless efforts of a mortified Secret Service to how Abraham Zapruder offloaded his historic roll of film, the movie swells with a gritty realism that is often lacking in the glossier, more casual glances at the assassination. While some criticized the movie for having no central character or narrative, the individual vignettes—particularly that of Oswald's overwhelmed brother Robert processing what Lee has done—are powerful enough to make it the cream of this particular crop.

Where the menagerie of assassination films grows dramatically more creative is in the sub-subset of *fictional* side stories—featuring completely made-up tales and characters loosely revolving around the assassinations. Yet, in a telling detail, this category is entirely dedicated to the JFK assassination (unless you count New York detective John Kennedy's railroad escapades in *The Tall Target*, which we examined earlier). One of the initial examples is *Flashpoint*—a 1984 film focusing on a pair of quasi-corrupt U.S. border patrol agents who blunder into an ongoing cover-up of the assassination 20 years later. Or is it? Quite literally, if you blinked at the wrong time in the final minutes of the film, you would never know the movie had anything to do with the assassination. In essence, it's the film's editor—using a couple of quick flashcuts to Kennedy's portrait at a key moment at the climax—who infers that a body the agents found buried in the sand along the border along with $800,000 was the actual assassin of the president.

Love Field takes a more artistic, if less exciting route. Featuring Michelle Pfeiffer as a Dallas housewife mesmerized by Jackie Kennedy, the story focuses on Pfeiffer's character embarking on an impulsive, if not illogical, cross-country jaunt to attend JFK's funeral. She winds up accidentally informing the FBI of a father's attempt to rescue his estranged young daughter that becomes a painful slog east for a white woman and a black man traveling through Jim Crow America. Pfeiffer's character misses the funeral and they all wind up getting caught in a fairly predictable conclusion, but Pfeiffer did earn an Oscar nomination for her performance.

The Bystander Theory and *The Umbrella Man* take similarly winding paths around the Kennedy assassination. The former is a complicated bit of work, centered around a lost film made of the assassination that becomes a MacGuffin after its owner dies and his granddaughter gets pulled into a nefarious (though charmingly low-level) plot to find it in the hope that it might prove that other shooters were involved. *The Umbrella Man* takes a more grounded, melodramatic approach when a man whose son was killed in an accident becomes obsessed with the Kennedy assassination in his grief and cooks up a theory about a man holding an umbrella at the foot of the grassy knoll as the motorcade drives by. These films get extra credit for spicing up ordinary stories with real-life substance, but both wind up feeling like Hallmark movies with a dash of paranoia sprinkled on top.

Paranoia defines *Interview with the Assassin*, a low-budget potboiler about a dying man who hires a neighbor to film his confession that he's the one who shot JFK from the grassy knoll. Merging a fictional Kennedy assassination tale with the found-footage style of *The Blair Witch Project* and *Paranormal Activity*, it's an entertaining aside that's really only satisfying if you interpret its somewhat ambiguous ending in the right way.

Probably the best known of this batch of fictional side stories is 1993's *In the Line of Fire*, which cleverly manages to incorporate both the JFK and Lincoln assassinations. Clint Eastwood stars as a veteran Secret Service agent haunted by his failure to protect Kennedy when he was part of the president's detail in Dallas. He's lured into a cat-and-mouse game with a would-be assassin of the current (fictional) president. The villain, played to perfection by John Malkovich, is obsessed with the JFK shooting and baits Eastwood into trying to catch him. "Why not call me Booth?" he asks Eastwood over the phone early in the film. "Why not Oswald?" Eastwood counters. "Because Booth had flair and panache ... the leap to the stage after he shot Lincoln." Henceforth, Malkovich is referred to as "Booth" by the law enforcement officials pursuing him.

Also tying both assassinations together, believe it or not, is the farcical 2001 comedy *Zoolander*. A dimwitted fashion model, played by Ben Stiller, is drawn into a plot in which he's brainwashed to become an assassin. It's explained away in the screwball logic of the film that models have always been trained as assassins. Booth, we're told, was the first model/actor, manipulated to shoot Lincoln by the fashion industry in an attempt to keep clothing manufacturing costs down by preserving slavery. And while Oswald certainly wasn't a model, the movie posits, two well-dressed guys on the grassy knoll were—killing JFK because of a trade embargo he'd recently installed on Cuba that halted the shipment of specialty slacks.

As you can see, several of the fictional accounts of the assassination do tend to, consciously or unconsciously, lean toward conspiracy. But before we get to that portion of the film library, there's one more tangent we must explore. And "tangent" is an appropriate word for the bouquet of films that introduce time travel as a plot device to say something about the cultural ripple effect of assassination.

Though it's worth noting that there are no time travel films about the Lincoln assassination. It's understandable, since by the point at which time travel became a film trope, the Lincoln assassination was more than a century old, and its day-to-day impact didn't feel quite as immediate or powerful. But in reality, altering that event almost certainly would have had a larger impact on American history than saving Kennedy, particularly in terms of civil rights and racial equality. In essence, consider the alternative path of history if Lincoln's merciful approach had defined Reconstruction and prevented decades of further conflict, enriched racism, and cultural entrenchment.

Both *Timequest* and *Running Against Time* took a sci-fi swing at the same piñata, opining on how both America and the world would have been better had Kennedy remained president. *Timequest* goes full alternate universe, with a time traveler from the future arriving in Dallas the morning of the assassination to show JFK and Jackie what was about to happen, thereby altering the future. From there, things get a bit silly. Bobby Kennedy winds up in a gunfight with potential assassins on the grassy knoll, the Cold War is called off, and when JFK dies of natural causes in the year 2000, he's buried on the moon in a lunar colony that bears his name.

Running Against Time goes the H.G. Wells route, concluding that a significant historical event like this simply can't be stopped. And fate/destiny steps up to thwart our heroes' well-meaning plan to travel back to save Kennedy and prevent the United States' decade-long quagmire in Vietnam.

Pulpy as this idea sounds, it was alluring enough for Stephen King to take a whack at it. His novel *11-22-63* was developed into an eight-part Hulu series featuring James Franco as a schoolteacher sent back through a "rabbit hole" to prevent the assassination for basically the same general reason as the previous two films. And, predictably, he runs into the same problems. "If you do something that really fucks with the past," a character warns him at one point, "the past fucks with you." It's certainly the best of this bunch, leading to a *Twilight Zone*–twist in which saving JFK actually makes things worse.

While King's version does ultimately decide that Oswald acted alone, many of its initial episodes are spent on Franco's character trying to answer that question. It was an interesting and necessary bit of subtext, since by the time King wrote his story, conspiracy theories dominated the assassination topic. Primarily with Kennedy, but not exclusively.

The echo of conspiracy and paranoia began to seep into the film industry in general throughout the 1970s. And it didn't take long to adapt that sensibility into the death of JFK. The first film to tackle the idea that Oswald wasn't the lone gunman hit theatres in November of 1973, coinciding with the tenth anniversary. *Executive Action* features Burt Lancaster as, for lack of a better term, an assassination coordinator for a collection of rich white men who fear Kennedy will stop them from their mission to eliminate minorities and shrink the world's expanding population. After walking his benefactors through a slideshow of each presidential assassination attempt, Lancaster gradually begins putting together a plan for Kennedy's.

None of the characters portrayed in the film are framed as real people, nor does their motivation trace back to any real-world analog. "Although much of this film is fiction," a prologue voiceover announces, "much of it is also based on documented historical fact. Did the conspiracy we describe actually exist? We do not know. We merely suggest that it could have existed." If that logic has you scratching your head, you aren't the only one. "They don't seem to understand," film critic Roger Ebert noted in his review, "that showing something as it could have happened doesn't mean it did."

Four years after *Executive Action*, the Lincoln conspiracy idea got its turn. The ironic thing is that Lincoln's assassination was, without question, a conspiracy. So really, any movie about it technically qualifies, even if it's not introducing new ideas or controversial theories. *The Lincoln Conspiracy* suggests an entirely different conspiracy that envelopes the one we know about. In this one, powerful players within the federal government secretly knit together a plot to remove Lincoln from office before his forgiving attitude for reunification, in their view, would ruin everything.

The premise tracks a fringe theory that John Wilkes Booth wasn't ultimately hunted down and killed by federal troops. That man, the story goes, was actually a Confederate spy named James Boyd, who happened to look just like Booth and was sent by the conspirators to kidnap Lincoln after the play at Ford's Theatre on April 14. But Booth beats them to the punch, shooting the president on his own while Boyd was waiting in the wings to kidnap him. This shifts the plotters into damage-control mode to cover their tracks. They send Boyd out to silence Booth, but instead, Boyd is killed by the cavalry hunting Booth, which mistakes him for the assassin. The plotters stick with the story that it was Booth who was killed, and they consider the case closed. Booth, meanwhile, quietly escapes and lives a long and full life—possibly even touring the country after his death as a preserved mummy in a carnival sideshow. Almost hard to believe why this would be considered a fringe theory.

The only hanging thread was the diary that Booth kept, eventually found with 18 pages missing. *The Lincoln Conspiracy* concludes that in those pages, Booth implicates all the conspirators, and therefore the pages were removed and destroyed before the discovery of the diary was made public.

The Walt Disney Company provides another, slightly less nefarious take on those missing diary pages. *National Treasure 2: Book of Secrets* opens with Booth and co-conspirator Michael O'Laughlen visiting a distant relative of protagonist Ben Gates (played by Nicolas Cage) on the evening of the assassination. Booth shows ancestor Gates a cipher written in his diary and asks him to crack it. The plan is that the cipher will lead a Southern extremist group to the legendary temple of gold, where it will be able to access the supply and reignite the Confederacy with enough funding to win the war. Booth leaves to go shoot Lincoln, but when Gates's ancestor realizes that's what's at stake, he tears the missing pages from the diary and throws them into a fire before being killed himself. When a fragment of the missing pages turns up 140 years later, it implicates the Gates family in the conspiracy and leads Cage and his companions on a knockabout of riddle-solving and derring-do through a gauntlet of national historic sites. One of those stops is a secret room deep within the Library of Congress in which they discover the "President's Book," filled with details about the biggest secrets in American history. Naturally, as they scroll through the pages looking for the clue they need to lead them to the next scene, they breeze by a section about the Kennedy assassination. What was in that section remains unexplained, with the possibility of conspiracy hinted at, but ultimately left untouched.

Oliver Stone's 1991 epic *JFK*, on the other hand, does a running cannonball into the deep end of the conspiracy pool and, consequently, is the most recognized of any of its assassination movie brethren. Technically, the narrative propulsion is driven by New Orleans District Attorney Jim Garrison's investigation of the assassination and eventual prosecution of a local businessman's involvement. But what viewers remember is the miasma of possible (and in some cases, contradictory) conspiracy theories portrayed.

Say this for *JFK*—it's one of the most gripping, compelling films ever made. Culling together a revered cast of Hollywood all-stars, it reeks of authenticity and quality, garnering eight Academy Award nominations, including Best Picture. Its editing style is unlike anything seen before, mixing together real footage with sections filmed for the movie so that the difference is often unnoticeable. Unfortunately, that's a fitting allegory for the entire film—mixing reality and fantasy to the point you're not sure which is which. It never maintains anything beyond a casual relationship with facts, and while it asks questions that deserve to be asked and presents motives and theories that may be plausible, it never truly settles on a singular thesis. Instead, it winds up with more of a Russian roulette approach to conspiracy: *Here are a half-dozen theories ... odds are one of them is probably right.* As Garrison himself—played by Kevin Costner—explains in the film, "We're through the looking glass here, people."

The Wonderland metaphor aside, all of these films do serve as something of a mirror. They reflect our cultural compulsion to absorb, understand, and relive these pivotal moments in our history. And the roster of films on each assassination are similar enough in volume and categorization to be remarkable.

The connections and coincidences go even deeper if one cares to look. For example, a handful of actors pop up playing characters in similar assassination movies, though on opposite sides of the aisle. The actor who played a grassy knoll shooter of Kennedy in one movie (John Anderson) plays Lincoln in another. JFK's father in one (Tom Wilkinson) plays Mary Surratt's lawyer in another. Oswald in one (John Pleshette) is Lincoln's secretary of state William Seward in another. And that's just to name a few in what's a curiously long list. Which, of course, doesn't mean much. Over a career, an actor will play a wide range of similar roles in similar types of movies. At the end of the day, it's just one more log of coincidence to throw on the fire.

So too are the strikingly similar approaches and legacies of the wide range of films dedicated to either the Kennedy or Lincoln assassinations. From straightforward re-enactments to examinations of supporting characters to dastardly plots and back again, it's unlikely Hollywood will ever tire of launching new narrative journeys into these two events.

Nor will these films cease to echo and reflect one another, just as the assassinations do.

9

PH Balance

Believe it or not, one of the most compelling connections between the Kennedy and Lincoln assassinations is one that doesn't make a lot of lists.

Dr. Matrix didn't catch it when he compiled his original collection, and it doesn't appear on the wrinkled gift shop poster that includes many less impressive entries. Even Buddy Starcher didn't mention it in either installment of his "History Repeats Itself" ballad. There's an explanation why it doesn't appear in any of these compendiums, which makes it all the more enticing. Ultimately, this connection is like a late-arriving guest to the party who might arguably be one of the most interesting people there.

After sifting through all the similarities between the assassins, the collateral damage, and the site of the assassinations, we're left with the most poignant stops on the respective journeys: where each president actually died.

Abraham Lincoln's unconscious body was carried out of the presidential box at Ford's Theatre by a makeshift cadre of theatre patrons, down the winding staircase, and out into the rainy spring night. Deciding he wouldn't survive the bumpy carriage trip back to the White House, the group needed a place to take the president so he could die in peace. He was ultimately carried across Tenth Street to a boarding house where, nine hours later, he would draw his final breath.

Ninety-eight years later, after the shots were fired in Dealey Plaza, the X-100 raced onto the freeway for a frantic four-mile journey to the nearest hospital. Kennedy was wheeled inside and doctors diligently worked on what they knew was a hopeless case before the president was officially declared dead 20 minutes later.

At first glance, there's no apparent connection between these two stories or places. Until, that is, you hear the names of the two sites.

Petersen House and Parkland Hospital.

P and H.

It's another letter play, though slightly more powerful than the cocktail of similarities between the number of characters in the key players' names. For all the actuarial possibilities of the length and structural similarities between names and places, the odds of two presidents dying in locations with names that began with the same two letters is incalculably low.

Which brings us to the elephant in the room. If, you may wonder, it's such an amazing coincidence, why didn't Dr. Matrix, Buddy Starcher, or the Historical Documents Company pick up on it? The simple answer is that the Petersen House didn't really get its identity cemented until relatively late in the game. Like Muhammad Ali and Kareem Abdul-Jabbar, it was known by another name for much of its history before settling on its ultimate identity.

For roughly the first century following the assassination, the Petersen House was referred to as "The House Where Lincoln Died," which sounds more like a Wes Craven movie than a tourist attraction. The shift to "Petersen House" was gradual and doesn't have a clear moment of demarcation in the building's timeline. But that shift clearly occurred *after* Parkland Hospital became known to the world.

The knee-jerk reaction of naysayers may be to suggest that, for that reason, this one shouldn't really count. That this coincidence was manufactured after the fact to fit the pattern, like pounding two disconnected puzzle pieces together with your fist. On the contrary, while the proper-name label of "Petersen House" didn't evolve right away, its point of origin is both genuine and unquestionably natural. There's really nothing else the building should or could be called. In fact, the naysayers' argument itself might provide an even more powerful testimony. To suggest that the National Park Service either consciously or unconsciously renamed one of its sites to better connect the Lincoln assassination to the Kennedy assassination would seem to be evidence of some higher power at work.

Let's start with the basics. The house was built in 1849 by a German immigrant named William Petersen. A tailor by trade who'd made a fortune making uniforms for military officers during the war, Petersen knew the four-story brick home was larger than his family needed, so he rented out empty rooms to boarders. This setup would continue for decades, reaching its apex during the Civil War when boarding houses, hotels, and apartments throughout the capital were filled to capacity by soldiers and visitors alike. As many as 21 people at a time lived in what was often colloquially referred to as "Petersen's boarding house."

As the gaggle of soldiers awkwardly carried the unconscious Lincoln across the street on April 14, there was a moment of peak confusion. The group decision was that Lincoln shouldn't be left to die on the floor of the box inside the theatre, but now what? He'd almost certainly perish on the carriage ride back to the White House, which seemed an equally undignified ending. It was at that moment that Charles Leale, the first doctor to treat Lincoln after the shooting, spotted a man standing in the front door of the Petersen House holding a single candle aloft, shouting, "Bring him here!"

That man was Henry Safford, a boarder at the house, who was taking a night off after several evenings of revelry and celebration of the end of the war. He'd been quietly reading when he heard a commotion outside and looked out the window to see the madness below. He came to the door just in time to decipher what was happening and the conundrum the makeshift group was facing. He quickly realized that the boarding house he was staying in would be a suitable option for the sanctuary they sought and invited them inside, forever cementing the Petersen House into American history.

As the group shuffled across Tenth Street and up the stairs toward the front door where Safford stood beckoning them, they grasped for and/or brushed up against an iron railing along the stairway. That same iron railing is there today. It's been restored a bit over the years, but visitors to the Petersen House can run their hands across the same piece of metal that anyone and everyone who entered the house that fateful evening would have touched. It is one of the few truly tactile historical connections one can make at any Lincoln or Kennedy assassination-related site or exhibit.

Yet it's not the only flavor of authenticity the Petersen House offers. While Ford's Theatre gets much of the attention, the Petersen House quietly offers an equal, if not more powerful experience. And authenticity is its biggest attraction. While the theatre was essentially entirely rebuilt in the years that followed the assassination, the core structure of the Petersen House is still exactly what it was in 1865, inside and out.

Standing in the middle of Tenth Street with your back to Ford's Theatre, almost everything you see is what the men carrying Lincoln saw that rainy night: the original brickwork, original window framing and, in some cases, original panes of glass. The woodwork around the doors. The door itself, in fact. The stairs leading up to the door are the only part of the exterior that are entirely unoriginal. They needed to be replaced after a wayward site-seeing bus crashed into them in what must have been a fairly hilarious incident in the 1920s.

The authenticity continues inside. The banister, railing, and null post on the staircase leading to the second floor are all the same, and can be touched just as they were that April night. Unlike at most historical sites, the sense of history inside the Petersen House is both tactile and auditory. "As visitors are walking along, they can hear the squeaks of the floorboards," says David Byers, Supervisory Park Ranger at the Ford's Theatre National Historic Site. "Those are likely the same squeaks that they heard as they were carrying Lincoln through."

As you follow their footsteps on the same creaky floorboards down the narrow first-floor hallway, you quickly reach what is charmingly referred to as the "Death Room." Here, Lincoln was laid down diagonally onto a bed too small for him, nestled beneath the crook of the staircase above.

While expanded and embellished in some of the paintings and portrayals over the years, you realize immediately that this monumental spot in American history is no bigger than a college dorm room. It's fifteen feet by nine feet, with oatmeal-colored wallpaper above a thin red rug on the floor and a few bland pictures hung on

The haunting "death room" within the Petersen House the night of the Lincoln assassination. Today it provides perhaps the most authentic—and powerful—visitor experience of any assassination historic site (The Miriam and Ira D. Wallach Division of Art, Prints and Photographs: Picture Collection, The New York Public Library).

the wall. Altogether, it's a startlingly ordinary place for the most revered American president to leave this world.

What sometimes gets lost in the stories of the long night ahead is that the bed in which Lincoln died rightfully belonged to someone else. Not Henry Safford, who'd beckoned the entourage inside, but William Clark, a former Union soldier who at that time was working as a clerk in the adjutant general's office. He was renting the back room beneath the stairs but was out that evening, celebrating the end of the war just as Safford had been much of that week. While Clark plays little to no role in the story, it's fascinating to imagine his reaction upon returning the following morning and being told why his room was such a mess: "Wait—*what*?"

By most accounts, he returned just after the president's body had been removed. He would spend the next several days dealing with visitors coming into his room to see the place where Lincoln had died. In some cases, they took swatches of wallpaper or some other souvenirs from the room with them. Clark himself was a bit less sentimental. That night, he slept on the same bed, beneath the same covers under which Lincoln had perished that morning.

The furnishings that have been displayed in the Death Room over the years have never been the originals, though some of those original pieces still exist. The actual bed in which Lincoln died, for instance, was eventually auctioned off and is now displayed at the Chicago History Museum. So while the bed that rests behind a comfortable layer of plexiglass at the Petersen House isn't the original, it is a period piece from the same era, providing just enough flavor for visitors to appreciate what it represents.

With or without the bed or other furniture or decorations, the Death Room has an undeniable austerity. "It's powerful just to know that these are the very walls that contained this monumental event," Byers says. "And to picture all of the people that were there at the time, many of them important historical figures in their own right. Also, I think for many people it's very evocative of situations where families get together when there's a loved one who's not doing well and is not going to survive. There's the weight of that moment you can feel there much more than you necessarily do at the Ford's Theatre site."

Just like most of these structures, the Petersen House did go through a period following the assassination in which it (or rather, its caretakers) wrestled with its own importance. When William Petersen and his wife died in 1871, their children auctioned off the furniture from the Death Room, but kept the property and continued to operate it as a boarding house for another seven years. They then sold it to Louis Schade, who used it as a both a home and an office for a small newspaper he operated. Throughout this era, visitors would often knock on the front door and ask to see the Death Room, particularly after a marble tablet reading "The House Where Lincoln Died" was attached to the exterior of the house in 1883. Reportedly tired of all the attention his home was getting, Schade moved out a decade later and leased it to the Memorial Association of the District of Columbia—a small group of civic-minded citizens out to ensure that historic buildings in the capital were preserved.

It was right around this time that the character who, for better or worse, would become the champion of the Petersen House emerged out of the west like a carnival barker thrown out of a prairie town for selling snake oil.

Osborn Hamiline Ingham Oldroyd is a fascinating anagram to the history of the Lincoln assassination. Starting with his own name, in fact—the first letter of each word deliberately spells out "Ohio," the state of his birth. He became ensorcelled with Abraham Lincoln during the 1860 election, a feeling that only deepened over the next few years as Oldroyd fought for the Union in the Civil War. Along the way, he began collecting any and all Lincoln artifacts he could find, from campaign buttons to posters to a baby cradle owned by the family to a train rail supposedly split by Lincoln himself.

At a memorial service for Lincoln in 1880, Oldroyd was struck by the idea of putting his collection—now totaling about 2000 pieces—on display. Shortly after, the opportunity of a lifetime opened up. Robert Todd Lincoln was looking for a new renter to live in and care for the Lincoln family home in Springfield, Illinois, in which the president and his family had lived prior to moving into the White House. Oldroyd seized the chance and moved into the house, along with his vast collection of Lincolnalia. Once he was established in the home, his natural tendency toward self-promotion took over. Giving himself the nickname of "Captain," he'd allow visitors to enter the home and see his collection for a small fee. Robert Todd Lincoln didn't care for the sideshow-like techniques, but took no serious issue with the setup, at least not until Oldroyd started falling behind on his $25 monthly rent. Making matters worse, Robert heard rumors that Oldroyd was further lining his pockets by cutting off parts of the curtains, wallpaper, and flooring and selling them to collectors.

Robert, who would eventually refer to Oldroyd as a deadbeat, considered suing him, but feared the publicity that would draw. Instead, he washed his hands of the matter and donated the house to the state of Illinois under the proviso that the state maintain the home and never charge visitors admission to see it. While Captain Deadbeat lost his income source, the state did invite him to stay in the home as a curator and offered him a $1,000 annual salary.

The setup lasted until 1893, when a newly elected Democratic governor kicked Oldroyd out in favor of a friend. But Oldroyd, just as he had 10 years earlier, saw and seized opportunity. Whether he initiated the discussion is unclear, but the Memorial Association back in Washington asked Oldroyd to move his collection into the House Where Lincoln Died. Perhaps appropriately, on his way out of Springfield, Oldroyd added to his collection by taking several items from the Lincoln home that weren't rightfully his—most notably Mary Lincoln's cast-iron cookstove.

In 1896, his collection was put on display in the Petersen House. Again he charged visitors admission, and when the federal government purchased the home from the Schades that same year, Oldroyd was permitted to stay on. For the next 30 years, the Petersen House was Oldroyd's domain—he and his family living upstairs, his vast and constantly growing collection on display on the first floor. Exhibits even filled up the Death Room, where Oldroyd had the back wall removed and pushed back in order to make more space.

So while Ford's Theatre teetered on the brink of oblivion across the street, the Petersen House carved out a nice little niche for itself as a tourist attraction and spot of significance. Oldroyd's lifelong commitment received formal recognition in 1926 when the federal government—steered by the involvement of Congressman Henry Rathbone—purchased his collection for $50,000. Oldroyd moved out of the home he'd lived in for three decades, but was given a key to the Petersen House, with the open invitation that he could return any time he liked—a reward for the years of service he'd provided.

Even as he reeled in more cash than most Americans at that time would see in their entire lives, Oldroyd martyred himself a bit. He pointed out that he'd actually had offers for more than $100,000 for the collection. He sacrificed the money, he explained, for the greater good. "He truly believed this collection is something that should be kept up in perpetuity and should be in safe hands," Byers says. "He was concerned that a private collector would wind up piecing it off and selling it bit by bit. Or wouldn't allow people to come in and appreciate it."

For all of Oldroyd's slightly sketchy practices, without him, it's possible that both the Petersen House and Ford's Theatre might have faded away into obscurity and destruction. He rolled into town with an out-of-the-box appreciation for Lincoln and his assassination that was ahead of its time, and this foresight brought value to both historic locations in a period when little was to be found. Oldroyd died in 1930 and never got to see how the sites would grow in prestige and appreciation. But you can just picture his tight lips cracking into a small smile beneath his well-manicured white mustache were he to see what Tenth Street looks like today. In some ways, there's a little bit of Osborn Oldroyd in every Lincoln souvenir shop and t-shirt stand.

In 1932, Oldroyd's collection, by now filling every nook and cranny of the Petersen House, was moved across the street to Ford's Theatre as it began to transform into the historic experience it is today. As has become a repeating refrain throughout these stories, the Smithsonian had an opportunity to snag some of Oldroyd's loot, but decided that his collection was, in their words, "of no practical value." While it's important to keep context in mind when looking back on these tales, it's hard not to picture the dazzling display of top-shelf assassination artifacts the Smithsonian could have today had its leadership made different decisions over the years.

After Oldroyd's collection moved across the street, a movement began to restore the Petersen House back to the way it looked in 1865. It would take about 30 years and a couple of renovation projects to get there, but by the early 1960s—just a few years before Ford's Theatre would embark on a similar project—the Petersen House was returned to factory settings. As it did, a silent connection began to develop between it and Ford's Theatre. Always subtly tied together, their historic legacies began to merge in a more official sense as visitors started to define the two locations as *one* of the most interesting attractions in the capital.

Over the remainder of the century and beyond, rarely would visitors stop by one location without visiting the other. As part of Ford's

Theatre's 2009 upgrade, for the first time both attractions were included as part of a single ticket purchase. Technically, you could skip the Petersen House if you're in a hurry, since you would get the entire story through the exhibits' corresponding narratives and the ranger presentations at Ford's Theatre. "But you would miss out on an encounter with something authentic and genuine in experiencing that space and the weight of it," Byers says. "And there's something about standing by that bed. Even though you're separated by a piece of glass and it's not even the original bed, there's a connection that most people seem to feel. You feel the weight of that moment."

And, quite possibly, the weight of another moment that potentially slathers an additional layer of spooky atop the location. Believe it or not, the Petersen House has its own version of Ford's Theatre's *Marble Heart* story—an anecdote of morbid foreshadowing that, if true, would indeed seem to indicate that something beyond our comprehension played a role in the story.

Let's start with the parts that we know are true. Ever since Ford's Theatre had become a theatre, actors would often stay at the Petersen House for the duration of the show they were performing in. While there, they'd have scripts delivered to them by theatre staff. That's what William Ferguson, a part-time actor and callboy, says he was doing in March of 1865 on a routine trip across the street—bringing scripts to actors John Matthews and John McCullough, who were staying at the Petersen House while performing in *The Apostate*.

When Ferguson arrived, the two actors were visiting with another actor friend of theirs who was also in the play. As the three men lounged in the back section of the house that, in a month's time, would become known as the Death Room, Ferguson noticed John Wilkes Booth smoking a cigar while relaxing on a small bed tucked beneath the staircase. The same bed where, in just a few weeks, Abraham Lincoln would die.

Before we let reality take the mike, let's ponder the possibility of this story being true. Booth would frequently visit Matthews, who often rented a room in the Petersen House. Therefore, the odds of Booth setting foot inside the Petersen House for this purpose seems quite likely—which, in and of itself, is enough to provide a bit of a chill. It's his winding up in the back bedroom and taking such casual comfort on the bed in such close narrative proximity to the bed's moment of fame that makes the story sparkle.

Picture the assassin leaning back and relaxing on that bed, having no idea that just a month later the president he despised so much would lie dying on that same spot due to the actions of said assassin himself. More than Lee Harvey Oswald writing a letter to John Connally, more than Booth pointing at Lincoln on stage, this is next-level creepy. This is the point we've reached a handful of other times along this journey: the point where coincidence ceases to be coincidence and demands to be considered something else.

Okay, now let's let reality have its turn. While it is absolutely possible that Matthews was renting a room at the Petersen House at this time, there's no evidence to prove it. The origin of the story itself is a bit wobbly, since it didn't surface for nearly 50 years. It's fair to suggest that if this story were true, someone (Ferguson, Matthews, or McCullough namely) would have made the connection almost immediately and the tale would have quickly become legend.

Ferguson himself is probably the weak link in the credibility of the whole thing. He is, as Byers likes to call him, the Forrest Gump of the Civil War. This is one of several stories he would tell in which he just happened to be in attendance at significant moments of the era, many of which have been proven not to be true. (For example, that he'd snuck into the Petersen House through the basement on the night of the assassination in order to see the dying president.) To be fair, Ferguson was definitely at Ford's Theatre during the assassination, and Booth rushed by him in his race offstage after the shooting. In fact, that afternoon, Ferguson had a drink with Booth at the Star Saloon next to the theatre, not knowing what the assassin had planned for that evening.

The tale of Booth lounging on Lincoln's death bed doesn't emerge until 1915, when Ferguson, who by now had established a successful acting career, was promoting a film in which he portrayed Lincoln. He also recounted the story for a book he wrote in 1930. "This is just one of the claims," Byers says, "that feels that it just too neatly fits into his pattern of 'Guess what—I was there and this amazing thing happened to *me*.' But still, there's nothing about it that is implausible. It's certainly possible."

An assassin lying on the spot where his victim would eventually die seems about as likely as an assassin dying at the same location his victim did. Which is exactly what happened at the other PH in our story.

***

With each of the assassination sites we've explored thus far, there's been a potential historical tangent in which the site doesn't become a site. At least not officially. And visitors and curators often comment on how things might have been different if that appetite for historic recognition had never come around.

That's what happened with Parkland Hospital.

Twice in that fateful weekend in November of 1963, it was the center of the world. On Friday afternoon and Sunday morning, respectively, President Kennedy and his assassin were each rushed to the hospital and eventually declared dead. But for all the drama and importance, Parkland Hospital never was and never will be a spot for tourists to visit—unless they have a medical ailment, of course. The hospital took that alternate path away from recognition immediately following the assassination and has stayed on it ever since.

Not that the rest of the world has figured it out yet. As the anniversary of the Kennedy assassination rolls around every November, Parkland gets inquiries from media outlets across America and around the world, looking to sprinkle a little extra flavor on their retrospective pieces. "Everybody wants to see Trauma Room 1," says Director of Corporate Communications April Foran. "It doesn't exist."

Trauma Room 1 was the small, green-tiled chamber where the president was examined and officially died. As Foran intimates, it's no longer there. It's parts and pieces do still exist, but unless you can somehow get access to a super-secret underground bunker in Kansas, you'll never get to see them. But we'll get to that.

Aside from black crepe hung on the door on the morning of Kennedy's funeral (and a small lock installed on the door for when the room wasn't in use to keep out the curious), nothing ever marked

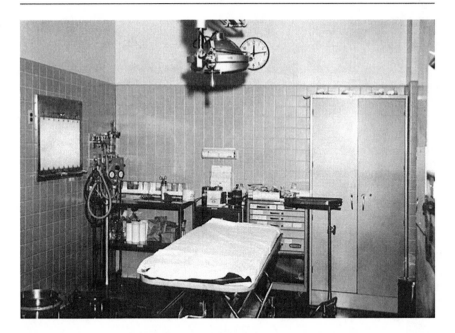

Parkland Hospital's Trauma Room 1 where President Kennedy was treated and pronounced dead (photo courtesy Parkland Health).

the spot while Trauma Room 1 was still in existence. For the next 10 years, it remained like any trauma room in any busy metropolitan hospital. In 1973, Parkland underwent a large renovation project that saw additional wings added onto the back of the building, where Trauma Room 1 had been located. The emergency department was moved and the spot at which the room was located became a part of the radiology wing. A small plaque was mounted on a pillar that's close to where the room was, simply reading "Original Site Trauma 1, November 22, 1963." In fact, the actual spot of the room was a few feet away, in what, in essence, was a closet.

In 2015, Parkland opened an entirely new building across the street from the one Kennedy was brought to, and the older structure became an outpatient clinic that gradually saw most of its remaining services transferred elsewhere. After sitting empty for several years, the old Parkland Hospital building was finally demolished in 2022. So even symbolically, nothing truly tactile remains of the site where Kennedy died.

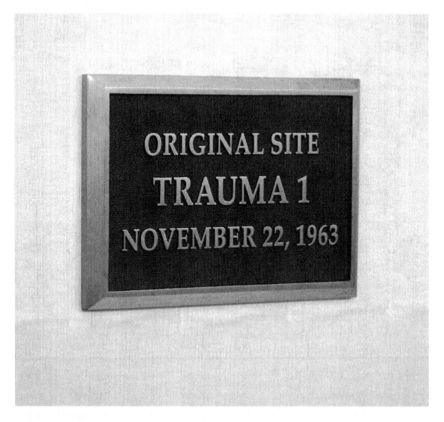

A plaque marked the spot where Trauma Room 1 was located after Parkland underwent renovations in 1973 (photo courtesy of Parkland Health).

This type of transition and expansion is nothing new for Parkland Hospital, which has been growing exponentially for well over a century. The original hospital opened in 1894 as a group of wooden frame buildings with the primary purpose of serving the poor. Its original name was less a commercial moniker meant to appeal to the masses than simply stating the facts: the hospital was built on land on which a park had stood. The hospital moved to a larger brick structure in 1914, and there it would stay until the fall of 1954, when the seven-story, T-shaped building that would become a part of history threw open its doors.

As Dallas grew, so did the hospital's need to expand. By the mid–1960s, three floors were added to the top of the structure, followed by the large remodeling of the back of the building a decade later which removed Trauma Room 1. But don't mistake this expansion for callousness. It's not like Parkland Hospital didn't appreciate the historical significance of what happened within its walls. A display was installed near the administration offices with a photograph of Kennedy, the seal of the president, and a large bust of Kennedy created by a local artist. That display remained in place for decades, then shifted to the new hospital in 2015 and remains in its lobby today.

The appreciation for the events of 1963 also emerged when the time came to remove Trauma Room 1. See if this sounds familiar: the hospital contacted the Smithsonian and asked if it would like to keep any part of the room or its equipment. Not surprisingly, considering its track record with these things, the Smithsonian said no. This time, though, it wasn't alone. The JFK Presidential Library also took a pass, but suggested that the contents should be given to the National Archives, primarily to keep them out of the hands of anyone who might seek to use them in an inappropriate way. The National Archives agreed to purchase the room and its contents, but shared the general concern about ghoulish opportunists. When you take the room apart, the Archives recommended in a letter just before the project began, keep it as low-key as possible to prevent souvenir hunters from stealing anything.

Trauma Room 1 was quickly and quietly dismantled on August 17 and 18, 1973. Doors, cabinets, lights, ceiling tiles, and plumbing, even the corresponding dust and debris, were carefully packed into crates and barrels and moved to a National Archives storage facility in Fort Worth. In 2008, the remnants were transferred to an underground facility at the Lenexa Federal Records Center in Kansas. Which adds to the *Mission: Impossible* flavor of it all, but in reality the decision was less about security and secrecy and more about temperature and humidity control. But security was still a factor. Unlike much of the National Archives treasure trove of historical documents and artifacts, there would be absolutely no opportunity for access, photography, or research.

While the respect for history is admirable, the intensity taken to shield the items from the public seems a bit over-the-top considering

(a) some of the items put into storage weren't actually there in 1963 and (b) those that were there had continued to be used for 10 years after the assassination in the process of treating thousands of other patients.

One patient on which they weren't used was the second-most memorable in the hospital's history. After Lee Harvey Oswald was shot in the abdomen at point-blank range by Jack Ruby in the basement of Dallas Police headquarters 47 hours after Kennedy's shooting, the alleged assassin was raced to Parkland just as the president had been. As he was wheeled down the same, green-tiled corridor, he was very deliberately placed in Trauma Room 2 rather than 1. While many of the same doctors who had treated Kennedy would also treat Oswald, to have done so in the same room seemed utterly wrong. As it happened, Trauma Room 2, just a few feet away, is where John Connally had been treated after being shot by Oswald. Like Connally, Oswald managed to make it out of Trauma Room 2, but died in an upstairs operating room a little over an hour later.

Parkland also became the final stop for a couple of the assassination's other key characters. In late 1966, Jack Ruby would be admitted to Parkland and died of cancer a month later. As did Abraham Zapruder, the Dallas dressmaker who had filmed the most famous home movie in American history, after a bout with stomach cancer in 1970.

Parkland's lack of any major commemoration of the events of that November weekend may initially strike some as odd. But with some further thought, the reason becomes both clear and completely understandable. Much of the power you feel when you visit other assassination-related sites comes from the abrupt transformation of an ordinary place into one of extreme power and significance. Parkland already was that.

When the Kennedy limousine arrived, 23 patients were already being treated in the Parkland emergency room. In the hour and 41 minutes between the time that Kennedy arrived at the hospital and when his body was removed, seven more patients were admitted. Eighteen babies were born at Parkland hospital that day, and several others, just like the president, died there that day. Life and death occurred, and still occur at Parkland each and every day. John Kennedy obviously wasn't just any other patient. But the technical, medical aspect of what happened at Parkland was nothing out of the ordinary. Like all hospitals, Parkland Hospital was then and remains today a powerful place. Conversely, Parkland's polite, essentially unspoken decline of any major historical designation offers a glimpse at what might have been if Ford's Theatre had remained a warehouse or the Texas School Book Depository had been leveled for a parking lot.

To be clear, Parkland doesn't shy away from its place in history. In addition to the display in the lobby of the new facility, the Kennedy assassination story is featured prominently on the hospital's website. "It's part of our history, and we understand that," Foran says. "It was a day in our history that we'll never forget, and tragic for our country. But it doesn't define Parkland."

What does define Parkland and its role in the assassination is best reflected in a letter from hospital administrator C. Jack Price to the entire staff the following week, praising them for their calm and professional efforts amidst a maelstrom of pressure. "Our pride is not that we were swept up by the whirlwind of tragic history," he wrote, "but that when we were, we were not found wanting."

Indeed, the only ones left wanting are those searching for Trauma Room 1. Or, in a more philosophical sense, a balance of historical recognition within the PH connection.

10

Escape of the Assassins: The Board Game

Welcome to the exciting new board game that everybody's talking about and, thankfully, nobody's playing! For generally one player, with an option for five to ten co-conspirators who may or may not have plausible deniability.

Object

To escape the scene of a presidential assassination and get away with the crime of the century without somehow being despised by the nation as a whole and forever vilified by history. Literally no one has ever won this game, so good luck!

Equipment

- A six-sided die
- Your choice of token: horse, rowboat, bus, or taxi
- Some form of firearm
- Your cunning and guile (which, heads up, are nowhere near as sharp as you think)

Setup

Shuffle the deck of Bad Decision cards and the decks of Lucky Break and Tough Break cards and place them on their respective spaces on the board. Place your token at the site of the assassination.

Rules

You've just killed a president, so you're likely not going to be overly concerned with this part. Basically just roll the die, move your token through the streets of a major American city, across bridges, and into neighborhoods and houses while trying to foolishly convince yourself you can somehow get away with this.

All right, we have a couple of players pulling up to the board. Can we get your names? Oh, you want to use your full names? Weird, but go ahead.

We have John Wilkes Booth, a stage actor and white supremacist, and Lee Harvey Oswald, a book warehouse employee and communist. Odd professions and definitions of personality, but this game seems to appeal to that type.

Both of our players have just fired their respective weapons and put a bullet in the head of the president of the United States, so let's get started! Mr. Booth, why don't you go first.

Booth rolls a 3.

You drop your pocket-sized, one-shot derringer pistol on the floor of the presidential box at Ford's Theatre. With the long dagger you hold in your other hand, you filet the upper arm of a lunging Major Henry Rathbone, then vault over the railing of the box to leap

John Wilkes Booth, the first presidential assassin (Library of Congress).

nine feet to the stage. You shout "Sic Semper Tyrannus!" the motto of your home state of Virginia, which translates to "Thus always for tyrants!"—which Brutus shouted after assassinating Julius Caesar. It's a bizarrely dramatic choice to start the game, especially since it helps the 1,700 people in the theatre clearly identify you as the assassin. And yet that choice still makes more sense than Virginia adopting the phrase as its state motto in the first place.

You run backstage and out the back door, then leap onto the horse you'd had a stagehand hold for you while you ran inside to alter American history. You gallop off into the night toward the Navy Yard Bridge, which will take you out of Washington.

Not a bad surge out of the gate for Mr. Booth. But uh-oh, looks like you landed on a Tough Break square. Go ahead and pick up a card off the stack there … oh, shoot. Looks like in your dramatic leap to the stage, you broke your leg—unexpected and yet totally predictable. Wonder if that'll come back to haunt you later in the game.

Oh, and what's this? Looks like you also drew a bonus Destroy an Innocent Bystander's Life card. Turns out that Ned Spangler, the guy you'd asked to hold your horse, will wind up going to prison for four years for it. Rough way to kick things off.

Mr. Oswald, let's see if you can get off to a better start.

Oswald rolls a 4.

You just fired three shots from the corner window of the sixth floor of the Texas School Book Depository. Rather than the "Sic Semper" center-stage approach, you open with a sneakier gambit. You run 96 feet from your makeshift sniper's nest to the other end of the sixth floor and hide your rifle among the stacks of boxes.

You start down the creaky wooden steps of the back stairway toward the building exit … but what's that sound? Uh oh—before you can reach the first floor, you hear footsteps racing up the stairs toward you.

Looks like your next turn could be your last one.

Lee Harvey Oswald, the fourth presidential assassin (Lyndal L. Shaneyfelt Collection/The Sixth Floor Museum at Dealey Plaza).

Booth rolls a 2.

You race your horse through the streets of the capital with no one on your tail, but with the understanding that you have to stay ahead of the news of your dastardly deed. You reach the Navy Yard Bridge, about three miles away from Ford's Theatre, at 10:45 p.m.

But whoops—the bridge closes every night at 9, and no one is allowed to enter or leave Washington until morning. And you're all in on this exit strategy: you don't have an alternate route out of town if you can't cross here.

However, you've landed on a Lucky Break square. Go ahead and draw your card. Ah, yes. You innocently tell the guard you didn't realize the bridge closed so early and ask him to make an exception and allow you across. With no way of yet knowing that the president has just been shot and his assassin is on the loose, the guard cuts you a break and allows you to cross the bridge.

You do so and are now out of the capital and free to escape through the Maryland countryside under cover of darkness.

Good fortune certainly smiled on Mr. Booth that turn. Let's see if Mr. Oswald can draft off some of that luck on his second roll.

Oswald rolls a 5.

Hearing hurried footsteps racing up the back stairway toward you, you duck through the door to the second floor. Right near that door is another, leading into a small lunchroom. You cut through there and stop at the vending machine for a Coke and a smile.

Uh-oh. As you do, you're confronted by the source of the footsteps on the stairs—a policeman who is now pointing his gun directly at you! Looks like your game might be over 90 seconds after it began.

The police officer is named Marrion Baker and he's about to accidentally become a part of history. He'd been driving a motorcycle in the motorcade and, after noticing a flock of birds suddenly taking off from the roof of the Depository as the shots were fired, raced into the building. He immediately ran into Roy Truly, the superintendent of the Depository, and asked him to lead him to the roof, from where he assumed the shots were fired. As the superintendent led him up the stairway, Baker caught a glimpse of you walking into the lunchroom and followed you there.

But, just like Booth before you, you've drawn a Lucky Break card on your second turn.

"Do you know this man?" Baker barks over his shoulder at Truly, still keeping his gun pointed at you. "Does he work here?"

Yes, Truly confirms, you work here. In the frantic seconds following the shooting, that's good enough for Baker, who understandably doesn't consider the coincidence that the assassin would also just happen to be a current employee. Helping your cause, you keep your cool, not appearing to be frazzled or out of breath. Baker lowers his gun and turns away from you, starting back up the stairs with Truly right behind him.

With an ice-cold Coke in your hand, you are now free to leave the building. You cut through the second-floor office space and make your way down to the main entrance of the building, which still won't be sealed for several more minutes. Just over three minutes after shooting the president, you're strolling along a Dallas sidewalk with no one pursuing or even suspecting you of your crime.

Yet.

Booth rolls a 1.

Having made it out of Washington and into Maryland, you pause and catch your breath at the previously arranged meeting point you'd designated with your partners in crime. After just a few minutes, you're joined by meek David Herold. He'd been the designated wingman for your fellow co-conspirator Lewis Powell, whose assignment was to kill Secretary of State William Seward in his home at the same time you were shooting Lincoln. Herold had waited outside while Powell went in, but took off when he heard the ruckus from Powell's ultimately unsuccessful attempt to stab Seward to death. Herold was able to talk his way across the bridge just as you were (suggesting that this was not an employee-of-the-month kind of night for the guard on duty).

Grab another token to move with you along every turn for the rest of the game. You, sir, now have a sidekick. A loyal Tonto to your homicidal Lone Ranger who will be able to help guide you through the countryside into safe haven. Or so you believe.

You and Herold stop by a nearby tavern to pick up supplies you'd sent ahead earlier which might come in handy. But while things appear to be humming along nicely, you've also reached a fork in the road in your journey. With your broken leg now throbbing with every gallop of your horse, you realize you need medical attention. The good news is you know someone who can help. The bad news is that the detour will take you well off course and soak up valuable time.

Mull over your pending decision while Mr. Oswald rolls the die.

Oswald rolls a 3.

You mosey seven blocks east through downtown Dallas and hop on a city bus. Snarled in the traffic jam prompted by the aftermath of the tragedy you just created, the bus crawls barely a tenth of a mile in five minutes. Like Booth, you know time is a factor, so you hop off the bus, walk a couple more blocks perpendicular to your original direction, and climb into a cab. You request to be taken across the Trinity River to Oak Cliff, the suburb four miles from downtown where you have rented a room in a boarding house.

Thus far your escape route looks like one of the silly dotted-line maps in the *Family Circus* cartoon strip. Like Billy catching pollywogs or Jeffy splashing in the bird bath on the way home from school, there hasn't been a whole lot of logic in what you've done to this point. You've been relying on reaction rather than thought. It's a bad habit to get into in this game and one you'll need to break quickly.

Booth rolls a 6.

You don't have a choice. Your leg hurts way too much to carry on this way. So you tell David Herold you need to sidetrack about 17 miles out of your way to Bryantown. There you'll find the home of Dr. Samuel Mudd, a friend you'd met the previous year (and who may have been involved in some of your early Lincoln kidnapping discussions).

You arrive at Dr. Mudd's house at 4 a.m. with a whole story about how you'd hurt yourself falling off your horse—not jumping to the stage after shooting the president. The assassination isn't discussed, and for decades after, Mudd's descendants would claim that you were actually in disguise and that the innocent doctor didn't know who you were or what you had done the whole time you were there.

Dr. Mudd treats your leg—you'd broken your fibula near your left ankle—and whips up some makeshift crutches for you to use. He allows you to spend the night. The next morning, as you rest, Dr. Mudd heads into nearby Bryantown to run some errands and discovers a cavalry unit preparing for a hard-target search through the area. He also hears the news of who they're looking for and why. Not at all a stupid man, Dr. Mudd puts two and two together.

Now you get to draw your second Lucky Break card of the game. Rather than waltzing over to one of the soldiers and informing him that the assassin they seek is dozing in his guest room just a few miles away, thereby avoiding any criminal charges and historic infamy, Dr. Mudd whistles right past the cavalry and returns home. He tells you what he discovered and orders you to leave—but not before giving you the name of a Confederate operative who will be able to aid you in your escape. He will say nothing to anyone about your visit to his home for a full day, allowing you to get enough of a head start to presumably escape to safety.

Along with your Lucky Break card, this entire subplot has earned you another Destroy an Innocent Bystander's Life card. Like Ned Spangler, Dr. Mudd will spend four years in prison for his impropriety. While it's fair to say that had you not broken your leg, we'd likely never have heard of Samuel Mudd, he's also not quite an innocent doctor who was imprisoned simply for helping an injured man in the night. Or at least he forfeited that claim when he opted not to turn you in (an action that looked even worse when his deeper relationship with you was uncovered).

In fact, while the origin of the phrase "his name is mud" technically doesn't stem from the tragedy of Dr. Mudd, the two are often mistakenly tied together. Consequently, the phrase endures as a symbol of his unfortunate and incidental involvement, along with the punishment he will ultimately receive for it.

Pick up a Create an Idiom card.

Oswald rolls a 2.

The cab takes you to Oak Cliff, where you hurry into your boarding house exactly 30 minutes after the president was shot. You grab a jacket and a small handgun and are back out the door three minutes later.

Where you plan on going from here is the most important part of your strategy in this game. And to this day, nobody knows exactly what the answer to that question is.

Booth rolls a 4.

The Confederate operative Dr. Mudd hooks you up with realizes the area is too hot to try to get you out right now. With soldiers and manhunters crawling everywhere, it's too risky to get you across the Potomac into Virginia until things cool down. Instead, he leads you to a pine thicket in the woods, where you and David Herold are instructed to hang tight. We'll see how things look in the morning, you're told.

Five days later, you're still there.

As you sit in the thicket, anxiously waiting and fearing discovery any moment, you're brought food and water, along with newspapers. To your surprise, you discover you're not the hero you thought you'd be, but have been deemed a villain and a monster. In response, you feverishly scribble out a counterpoint in a crazy, stream-of-consciousness series of entries in an appointment book you're carrying. In addition to embellishing the details of your adventure, you take a shot at justifying your murder of Lincoln with humdingers like "God simply made me the instrument of his punishment" and "I cannot see my wrong, except in serving a degenerate people."

While it feels like this is a lost turn, in fact it's been worth it. The searchers are unable to find you anywhere in Charles County and believe you've moved on. Eventually, they do too.

Oswald rolls a 4.

Wherever you may be going, you quickly start on your way, walking briskly in a southerly direction through the scruffy neighborhoods of Oak Cliff. While it feels like you have an unimpeded blue Texas sky ahead of you, little do you know that you're already being sought after. You're the only Texas School Book Depository employee who didn't return to the building after the assassination, and the police understandably find that a bit strange. Roy Truly—the building manager who saved your bacon with gun-wielding Officer Baker a few minutes ago—gives the police your name and description. Before you even made it back to your room, that description crackles over the radios of police cruisers all around Dallas.

Sure enough, as you scurry down the sidewalk along Beckley Avenue and then abruptly and randomly turn east on Tenth Street, a police officer in one of those cruisers spots you. Realizing you fit the description that was just broadcast three times in the past few minutes, he crawls his car behind you for a block or so. Then he pulls up beside you.

You're about to have your second encounter with a police officer in 45 minutes. You caught the luckiest of breaks last time. Wonder if your luck will hold out the second time around.

Booth rolls a 1.

Finally, after five days hiding in a damp, cold pine thicket, you get your chance to escape. In the cool spring darkness, you're led to a small rowboat along the banks of the Potomac. With a blanket over your head to cover the candle you need to read your compass bearings, you and David Herold begin perhaps the most important part of your journey to freedom. It's a triumphant moment in your escape, one that might just propel you all the way to victory.

But looks like you landed on a Tough Break square. You draw your card and ... uh-oh. After rowing along the water for five hours, you pull up on shore thinking you've reached Virginia. But it turns out you're *still* in Maryland. You got turned around and confused in the darkness and actually wound up farther away from where you want to go than you were when the night began.

With the frustration almost paralyzing, Herold leads you to the farm of another contact, who says you can stay but can't come in the house. Once again, you're forced to sleep outside, this time by a wooded creek, and have to stay until another opportunity arises. You'll wind up spending the next two nights here awaiting another chance.

Oswald rolls a 5.

J.D. Tippit, the police officer who just pulled his car up next to you, calls to you through the passenger window. We're not sure exactly what words are exchanged—likely he asks if you live nearby and where you're going. Your response must not do anything to allay his mild suspicion, because he gets out of the car to approach you.

Time for some quick thinking. Surely you must have anticipated this possibility and have a story prepared for who you are and where you're going. It likely wouldn't take much to tamp down the suspicions of Officer Tippit. There must be thousands of men who fit the description of the person the police were looking for. He has to be thinking that the odds of you being that guy are infinitesimal. Give him a decent, believable story and you're on your way.

Instead, nope. Time for a Bad Decision card. And it's a doozy.

You pull out the handgun you just picked up and fire four quick shots across the hood of the police car as Tippit rounds the front. They strike him in the chest and he falls to the ground by the left front tire. You start walking away, then turn back and fire one more shot for good measure, right into his head.

Clearly you must have felt like you had no choice, that your goose was cooked and your second murder of the lunch hour was the only way to go. As you walk away, you feel an instant rush of freedom, that you've bought yourself more time to continue along your haphazard escape route. Little do you know that a dozen witnesses around the neighborhood either saw the shooting or will see you leaving the scene, many of whom will be able to identify you in a lineup. In fact, one of them sitting in a nearby car hears you muttering under your breath as you walk away, reloading your pistol. "Poor dumb cop," you opine, not at all making you look any better.

Clearly, another Destroy an Innocent Bystander's Life card is in order. Tippit will be taken to nearby Methodist Hospital, where he will be declared DOA.

Meanwhile, you turn around, cut across the front yard of a nearby house—being seen by a couple more witnesses—and start up another street going the opposite direction you were going when Tippit stopped you. You're now headed toward the main drag of Oak Cliff.

That turn could have gone better.

Booth rolls a 5.

Your second attempt to cross the Potomac is a good news/ bad news scenario. The good news is that this time, you do indeed make it to Virginia. The bad news is it's not the right spot. David Herold, whose navigation skills have been less than optimal thus far, does redeem himself by going off to find another nearby Confederate contact he knows, who leads you both to the home of another doctor. This one, however, is not as friendly as Dr. Mudd (and, not coincidentally, won't wind up in federal prison). Now that more than a week has passed since the assassination, the news has spread, and he deduces exactly who you are and what you've done. He refuses you shelter and protection but points you toward a neighbor who might be willing to help—a black man who lives in a small cabin nearby. The neighbor wants nothing to do with you either, but after threatening him with the same knife with which you ripped up Major Rathbone's arm, he allows you to spend the night.

The next morning, you meet three Confederate soldiers, to whom you explain your situation. One of them knows a place where you might be able to stay if you cook up a better story than the one you've got going. He guides you to the farm of Richard Garrett, where you explain to the old farmer and his grown sons that you're a wounded Confederate soldier trying to make your way back home. He buys it and agrees to take care of you and David Herold for a couple days.

You have a hearty dinner and sleep in a comfortable bed for the first time in more than a week. It was the turn you were waiting for. After a couple rough breaks, it looks like you just might be able to win this game.

Oswald rolls a 3.

As you quickly move along the sidewalks, the cool fall air of Oak Cliff is pierced by the scream of police sirens rushing to the scene of a slain officer. There, witnesses are standing around eager to provide a detailed description of you. You're even hotter now than you were before.

You take off the jacket you were wearing and drop it in a parking lot you cut through, hoping to change your appearance ever so slightly and give you whatever marginal advantage you can get. (Though of course, once that jacket is found, searchers can more easily figure out what direction you're going.) About a half mile from where you shot Tippit, you walk west along Jefferson Avenue, the main thoroughfare of Oak Cliff, trying to appear casual.

Suddenly, you hear another burst of sirens and see several police cars tearing down the street. To avoid being seen, you step into the recessed area of the sidewalk by a store window and turn your back to the street. You try to appear as if you're carefully inspecting what's displayed in the store's window—shoes, as it turns out. It works. The police cars fly by you, continuing their search for Officer Tippit's murderer.

But uh-oh, time for another Tough Break card. Through the other side of the store window, shoe salesman Johnny Brewer can't help but notice you. For one thing, you're breathing heavily, your hair's messed up, and your shirt is untucked as you stare blankly into the window. More suspiciously, your attention is not at all on the parade of police cars screaming down the street, which would be the natural thing to look at for anyone who hadn't just shot a policeman to death and was now evading capture. It's almost as if, Brewer deduces, you were trying to avoid being seen. Brewer has been listening to the radio. He knows that the president has been shot and figures that police cars tearing around town might have something to do with it. His suspicion is piqued, especially when, as the police cars pass, you look over your shoulder to make sure the coast is clear, then step away from the window and continue down the street. Brewer steps out of the store to see what you do next.

Next to the shoe store is the Texas Theatre a small, single-screen cinema which had been a mainstay in Oak Cliff for nearly 30 years. With the box office cashier having stepped out of the booth to see what was going on with all the police car traffic, you slip into the theater without paying. Brewer, following you down the sidewalk, sees you do this, and tells the cashier about his suspicions of this shady character who just snuck past her. She promptly calls the police.

Had Brewer not noticed you through his store window, or had his suspicion not been so aroused—perhaps if he'd been helping a customer—things might have turned out differently. At the very least, you could have bought yourself more time inside the cool, dark shelter of the movie theater. Instead, as you settle in to your seat while *War Is Hell* flickers on the giant screen above, the Dallas Police descend upon the theater.

Booth rolls a 4.

Like Oswald, as you settle into relative comfort, the wheels toward your eventual discovery are turning.

The morning after arriving at the Garrett farmhouse, the 16th New York Cavalry, which has been hot on your trail for days now, is just a few miles away, banging on doors and following leads. One of those leads takes the cavalry just past the Garrett farm, and you and David Herold scamper into the nearby woods to hide as the thundering sound of dozens of horses rolls along the country road.

By now, the Garretts are catching on to your shenanigans, pretty sure that you're not actually an injured Confederate soldier. Garrett's oldest son John doesn't kick you out, but turns chilly, saying you'll need to stay the night in the small tobacco barn rather than inside the house. Beggars can't be choosers at this point, so you and Herold agree. Little do you know that John Garrett's suspicions are so sharp that he fears you two might abscond in the night, perhaps stealing some of their horses along the way. The Garrett sons secretly lock the door of the barn behind you. Unknowingly, a couple of random farmers have just captured the president's assassin.

Meanwhile, the cavalry tracks down the Confederate soldier who'd guided you to the Garrett farm. Not exactly a tough nut to crack, he immediately tells the soldiers where you are and offers to lead them to you.

At 2:00 that morning, the ominous drumbeat of galloping horses can be heard again. But this time they don't fade away into the gentle pulse of the spring night. They turn into the farmstead, and officers are pointed toward the tobacco barn, where the shady characters they're searching for are caged like animals. A long, awkward negotiation through the planks of the barn will ensue, which prolongs the inevitable. But through it all, you know there's no escape.

Game over.

Oswald rolls a 2.

As the movie plays on, police officers swarm the Texas Theatre. They cover every exit, fill the lobby, and stealthily begin to slip into the theater where you sit slumped in a seat with about a dozen other filmgoers. As it turns out, there are actually more police officers inside the theater than patrons. There is no possibility of escape.

The house lights come up and shoe salesman of the year Johnny Brewer points you out to them. They calmly approach you, slowly walking up the aisles of the theater. You try to play it cool, right up to the point when an officer asks you to stand up. You have one last Bad Decision card in your saddle bag as you mutter, "Well, it's all over now."

You leap to your feet, punch the officer right between the eyes, and reach into your pants to pull out your pistol. What exactly you intend to do with it is both puzzling and terrifying. By now even you understand you're outnumbered something like 15 to 1 by armed police and the only thing you could manage to accomplish would be to randomly kill a couple more innocent bystanders before being shot to death yourself. The officer you sucker-punched recovers and tackles you, and the two of you tumble into the seats as a football-like pileup ensues with other officers entering the fray. They claw the pistol out of your hand and handcuff you as you snivel, "Don't hit me anymore! I'm not resisting arrest! I want to complain of police brutality!"

A fittingly miserable end to a miserable game.

Postgame Analysis

Clearly, nobody won this game by completing its primary objective, but let's compare the numbers to see who performed better.

Mr. Booth, you managed to make it roughly 65 miles from the site of the assassination, stretching your escape over a span of 12 days. On a broken leg, no less.

Mr. Oswald, your escape attempt covered about five miles and lasted not quite 90 minutes. But to be fair, 100 years apart, this can't be an apples-to-apples comparison.

Booth's effort certainly looks better on the surface, particularly since he had no form of transportation other than horse and rowboat. On the flip side, he also didn't have to contend with the technical obstacles that Oswald did, namely police CBs and radio and television broadcasts, which enabled information of his actions to be widely circulated in minutes instead of days.

Another negative mark on Booth's score is the number of additional people he brought down with him. There were the four co-conspirators with whom he plotted the assassination, of course, who were ultimately captured and put to death. But along his escape route, he entangled and destroyed the lives of two primarily involuntary non-entities. That number could have been much higher had the government been so inclined to investigate and prosecute those that helped Booth escape as aggressively as those that plotted the assassination with him.

Conversely, while a couple of bystanders went to prison for crossing Booth's escape route, Oswald actually put somebody in the ground on his way out of town.

For all the collateral damage and additional shaky decisions, Booth clearly had a plan. He was relatively well funded, organized, and had assembled a network of support that, for the most part, came through for him. Were it not for a couple of unlucky breaks (quite literally, as a matter of fact), he just might have pulled it off.

Oswald on the other hand, had thirteen dollars, no support, and, even after more than a half century of exhaustive study, no discernible strategy. The best anyone's been able to offer is a theory proposed by a member of the Warren Commission counsel during its investigation of the assassination. It turns out Oswald had just enough money in his pocket to potentially purchase a bus ticket to Mexico. Based solely on hypothetical conjecture rather than evidence or testimony, the theory didn't make it into the commission's final report. And even if true, then what? Unlike Booth, Oswald had no connections or expectations of being able to disappear into a culture eager to protect him. He played this game in a completely reactionary fashion, like an assassin chicken with its head cut off.

So while nobody won, Booth lost a bit better, earning an honorable mention in a dishonorable game.

But remember, this game simply outlines the striking similarities in the assassins' escape attempts and where and how they came to an end.

There's one final, chilling coincidence connecting these two assassins and assassinations that we need to explore.

11

The Assassins' Assassins

"Crazy" is a tough word to define.

Even when you isolate it from the legal or medical arenas, where its use is frowned upon, it's a tricky term to put your finger on beyond describing rush-hour traffic or the amount of paperwork required to refinance your house.

Within the solar system of coincidences between the Lincoln and Kennedy assassinations, it's a particularly difficult condition to designate. On some level, anyone who would attempt to murder his own president has to have a little crazy flowing through him. Yet to casually tag either John Wilkes Booth or Lee Harvey Oswald with "crazy" feels like an exaggeration. "Misguided" or "pathetic," sure, but from what we know about them, neither immediately sparks the use of that word as a descriptor.

On the other hand, when we tick down to the final subset entry in the coincidences connecting the two assassins and reach the characters who provide the final act's plot twist … there. That's where we find the crazy.

Booth and Oswald's haphazard actions ultimately lead us to a pair of men who, I think we can all agree, really should not be a part of history. They were the wrong guys in the wrong place at the wrong time, and will forever be connected for exactly that. For committing an act that, however right it might have felt in the moment, is a permanent stain on history.

It's probably fair to ask the same questions about the appropriateness of using the word "crazy" with these two. It's not as if they escaped from an institution to do what they did or were unable to function as a part of society prior to doing it. (Come to think of it, one of them *did* escape from an institution, but that comes later.)

Perhaps the answer lies in linguistics. The true origin of the word "crazy" comes from the root "craze," which entered the English vernacular in the late sixteenth century and literally means "full of cracks."

Now we're talking.

Whatever medical and legal experts might decide about the mental capacity and functionality of the men who would become the assassins of the assassins, the one thing that's undeniable is that both Boston Corbett and Jack Ruby were full of cracks.

***

Before we hit the exit ramp to Crazytown, let's take a minute and really delve into the nooks and crannies of the coincidence that enables this to be a topic in the first place.

John Wilkes Booth and Lee Harvey Oswald were both killed at a time and place independent from the respective assassinations. Both had been discovered and, for all intents and purposes, captured by authorities. Then both were killed by a single person while surrounded by armed guards before either could be brought to trial.

By comparison, the assassins of James Garfield and William McKinley were each captured immediately at the sites of the shootings, while both were still armed. This was a context in which it would have been just as likely that one or both of them would have been killed themselves in the aftermath. But neither was. Similarly, of our closest modern equivalents—Squeaky Fromme, Sara Jane Moore, and John Hinckley (aka the Tony Orlando and Dawn of failed presidential assassinations)—none were killed on the spot by a Secret Service detail trained to do exactly that in this type of scenario.

Booth and Oswald did escape their respective scenes, which perhaps decreased the likelihood of immediate reactionary execution. Yet each of their escape routes (such as they were) ultimately led to a standoff that ratcheted up that likelihood once again.

We now simply accept that if anyone were to attempt to

176

assassinate an American president, that person would almost certainly be giving up their life in the bargain. There would be no capture or manhunt or trial or verdict. Whatever happened, the whole thing would be over in about nine seconds.

So it's fairly amazing to consider the odds of two separate assassins successfully committing the deed, fleeing a very public scene, and being tracked down without being killed ... only *then* to be killed at what would seem like the least likely moment in that timeline.

While there may be some level of mysticism tying these two shootings-after-a-shooting together, the more common thread is incompetence. In each case, the opportunity for the assassins to be shot themselves was made possible by poor decision-making by the officials in charge of bringing Booth and Oswald to justice or jurisprudence.

Let's start with Booth, whose escape attempt came to an end at the Garrett farm, in a tobacco barn surrounded by Union soldiers. Even though Booth was penned up inside the barn like a farm animal, the setting was not optimal for the soldiers. In the pitch darkness broken only by torches, none of them had a good view of Booth. Still, Booth was in big trouble and he knew it. Hobbling around on crutches and hopelessly outnumbered, Booth was ordered to come out of the barn or the soldiers would come in and get him.

In the first of a series of strange strategic decisions, the cavalry first sent one of the Garrett sons into the barn to try to talk Booth out. When that didn't work, they asked Booth to come out in 15 minutes or they'd set the barn on fire. With time running out, Booth shouted through the barn planks that his associate, David Herold, wanted to surrender. The barn door was opened and Herold was pulled out. Then, even with the initial deadline now passed, Booth was given a few more minutes to weigh his options.

As the waiting drew out, a peculiar sergeant in the group of soldiers named Boston Corbett volunteered to enter the barn and fight Booth mano a mano. Either he'd successfully take down the assassin or force him to use up his ammunition and distract him long enough so that the remainder of the cavalry could take him. Three times Corbett offered himself on this suicide mission and three times he was denied—a crucifixion allegory that, as we'll see, certainly wasn't lost on Corbett.

Once the cavalry's reset clock ran out, the order was given to set the barn ablaze to force Booth's hand. Starting a small patch of brush on fire at the back of the barn, the whole thing caught quickly and rapidly began to spread. One way or the other, Booth had a decision to make among three pretty lousy choices: surrender, kill himself, or come out of the barn fighting.

Explaining that God ordered him to kill John Wilkes Booth, Boston Corbett was a bizarre and troubled man who inserted himself into history—then vanished from it (Library of Congress).

And here's where a thin veil drops down over the events, blurring the view of what actually happened and why. Watching him through a gap between the planks of the barn, Corbett decided that: (a) Booth was about to start shooting at the soldiers from inside the barn, (b) Booth was about to make a break for the door and come out blazing, or (c) God ordered a hit.

Corbett leveled his Colt revolver at Booth and fired at the assassin. Corbett claimed he was aiming for his shoulder, but then Booth moved at the last moment. Coincidentally (or, of course, perhaps not), Booth was struck at almost the exact same spot that his own bullet hit Lincoln: on the rear left side of the head. It shattered Booth's vertebrae and severed his spinal cord.

"When the assassin lay at my feet, a wounded man," Corbett would later say, "and I saw the bullet had taken effect about an inch back of the ear, and I remembered that Mr. Lincoln was wounded about the same part of the head, I said, 'What a God we have.... God avenged Abraham Lincoln.'" Consequently, Corbett would earn the nickname of "Lincoln's Avenger."

Booth was dragged out of the burning barn and carried to the front porch of the Garrett home. There he lay paralyzed and semi-conscious for the next several hours. He finally died at dawn, never being forced to stand trial to explain or answer for his actions.

Initially, Corbett said he fired at Booth because God had told him to do it. Which, strange as it sounds, made sense for a man like Corbett. "Corbett was of the sort," the *Christian Advocate* would write, "who think that every thing that comes into their heads is inspired by God." Perhaps to help his case with those who may not have been as open to the idea of God ordering a soldier to open fire, Corbett's later explanation was a bit more secular. "It was not through fear at all that I shot him," he would say, "but because it was my impression that it was time for the man to be shot." Sort of like a movie director nudging his editor to pick up the pace of a climactic scene that was going on far too long. Corbett did say he wanted to prevent his fellow soldiers from getting shot (see his earlier offer to fight Booth, cage-match style). While his superiors were upset that Corbett's actions had prevented them from their primary objective of taking Booth alive, Corbett had not technically violated orders. No specific direction had been provided to the soldiers not to fire at Booth. It was another strategic oversight that might have altered the outcome.

But even if clear orders had been given not to shoot, it's very likely that all of this might have played out exactly the same way. Once Boston Corbett got it in his head to do something, consequences didn't matter.

Born Thomas Corbett in 1832, he was an English immigrant on his way to becoming a lifelong drunk after his wife and baby died in childbirth when he was 24. He worked as a hatter before the war and moved from city to city, going wherever jobs were available.

When he reached Boston, he joined the Methodist church and vowed to reform, giving up alcohol and dedicating his life to God. He changed his name to "Boston" in honor of the city where he altered his path, and even grew his hair long to better resemble Jesus Christ. When not haberdashering, Corbett was a street preacher: he'd set up a pulpit on a busy street corner and offer sermons to whomever passed by, whether they wanted to hear them or not.

It's often difficult to provide postgame psychological analysis of historical characters years later, but it's very likely Corbett suffered from mental problems long before the events that made him famous. The primary culprit may have been a result of his career as a hat-maker. In the nineteenth century, many who worked in this field suffered from exposure to the mercury used in the process of turning fur into felt. This exposure led to a smorgasbord of mental issues, most notably anxiety and depression. And, not-so-fun fact, therein lies the origin of the term "mad as a hatter." Combine this with his newfound and unrealistically intense dedication to scripture, and you have a recipe for problems. Exemplified by what happened next.

On a July day in 1858, Corbett was propositioned by a pair of prostitutes on the street. He turned them down, but was troubled that he was subject to such a temptation. In that moment of self-doubt, he turned to the Bible, specifically a phrase from the Book of Matthew, to guide his way: "And if thy right eye offend thee, pluck it out and cast it from thee...."

So naturally, he did what any man would do. He went home and cut off his testicles with a pair of scissors. Then he attended a prayer meeting and went out to dinner before eventually checking in to the hospital, where he was treated for a nasty infection and spent the next month recovering. Physically, at least.

Certainly there's no better place for a mentally troubled young man than the military, so when the Civil War began, Corbett enlisted in the Union army. While it may have seemed odd for such a religious-leaning person to embrace and participate in orchestrated mass murder, he claimed to say a silent prayer before every shot he fired: "May God have mercy on your souls."

In a fun ships-in-the-night subplot, Boston Corbett actually met

Abraham Lincoln while Corbett's regiment was briefly stationed in Washington in 1861. You can almost envision the historic weight of an otherwise pedestrian moment: the president shaking the hand of the man who would liquidate his own assassin almost exactly four years before it happened.

Corbett was a tough fit for the Army, often sanctimoniously reprimanding fellow soldiers and even superiors for using foul language or partaking in other unsavory behavior. He'd eventually be court-martialed for his righteous insubordination and mustered out of the military. But he rejoined shortly after. In 1864, he was captured by Confederate soldiers and held at the infamous Andersonville prison camp in Georgia for four months. There he led prayer services and funerals, both of which were in high demand at Andersonville. He also became quite ill himself. In fact, many of the ailments would linger for the rest of his life.

After the showdown at the Garrett farm the following spring, Corbett became something of a celebrity. He received fan mail and was frequently invited to headline church services and speaking engagements, where he'd tell his story of killing Booth. Mathew Brady, known as America's first photographer, took Corbett's picture—which was quite an honor at the time and reflective of his sudden social status and celebrity. "He has been greatly lionized," the Associated Press reported, "and, on the street, was repeatedly surrounded by citizens who manifested their appreciation of his services by loud cheers."

Many of those manifesting their appreciation longed to see the gun that Corbett used to shoot Booth, some even offering to buy it from him. But the gun was stolen from Corbett shortly after he'd used it, and to this day, no one knows what happened to it.

As the smoke of fame began to clear and America settled into its post-war existence, Corbett returned to the mercury-clouded world of hat-making. Naturally, he began to slide even further into madness. Most notably, now instead of simply vocalizing his objections over other people's actions or behavior, he began utilizing weapons. He'd occasionally whip out a pistol when agitated and wave it around at people, a practice which became more and more frequent.

It started just a few weeks after the shooting of Booth, when Corbett pointed his gun at an army sergeant during an argument.

An irrational sense of paranoia began to take over. He saw enemies everywhere, and eventually started carrying pistols at all times. Some of his worry was warranted, since he did receive menacing letters from Southern sympathizers who vilified Corbett for shooting Booth and threatened to kill him.

Corbett spent much of the 1870s traveling around the country trying to get work. Finally, giving up on hat-making, he put in a claim to an 80-acre farmstead near Concordia, Kansas, and decided to move there from Camden, New Jersey. Somehow not out of character, he opted to walk the 1,300-mile journey. He managed to make the first 100 miles almost entirely on foot before finagling a train ticket to get him the rest of the way to Kansas. There he built a dugout home into a hill and began life as a farmer.

But even living an isolated, apparently bucolic life, Corbett was still haunted by his mental issues. He filled his home with weapons and never allowed anyone inside. He'd get into arguments with people in town over seemingly innocuous offenses. In the fall of 1885, he fired shots at a few boys cutting across his property, which led to a criminal complaint for which he was put on trial. After being accused of lying while testifying, he pulled out a gun and began yelling at everyone in the courtroom, then fled back to his farm. When the local constable arrived the next day to take him into custody, Corbett pointed his rifle at him and said he wasn't going anywhere. Evidently deciding Corbett's lunacy was simply too much work, the constable left and the entire case was dropped. Frontier justice, baby.

Not that life as a farmer was going that well anyway. Even after receiving his military pension, by 1887, Corbett was struggling financially. An old army buddy got him a job as the assistant doorkeeper for the Kansas House of Representatives (begging the question of whether a doorkeeper truly needs an assistant). He began work and became something of a tourist attraction. People came to see the assassin's assassin and shake his hand. He even endeared himself to his coworkers, often helping out the janitorial and maintenance staff. All in all, it seemed like a pretty good gig for a 54-year-old guy coming into the twilight of a difficult life. But a month into the job, Corbett's demons surfaced once again.

One day as he was helping sweep a corridor, he heard a group of workmen joking and became convinced they were laughing at him. He came up to the group and pointed his pistol at the back of one of the workers. The men scattered in terror, fearing for their lives. As they did, Corbett simply holstered his pistol, picked his broom back up and started sweeping again. When someone else approached him shortly afterward to ask what had happened, Corbett pointed his pistol at him, as he did with a pair of friends who attempted to get an explanation. He was convinced they all were conspiring against him. Police eventually arrived, snuck up on him, tackled him, and carted him away to jail.

At a hastily put together sanity trial the next day, Corbett explained that members of a secret society that Booth had once belonged to were hunting him. The judge didn't buy it. He ruled Corbett was insane and a danger to those around him, then sent him to the Kansas State Insane Asylum in Topeka. Even institutionalized, Corbett remained a danger to those around him, at one point attacking a dining hall employee with a knife.

A year later, on a daily walk around the grounds with other patients, Corbett noticed a horse, tethered to a fence, that a young boy had ridden to visit the administrator's son, who lived on the grounds. Seizing the opportunity, Corbett broke from the pack, jumped on the horse, and rode away. His escape sparked quite a response, primarily because, in another fit of paranoiac delusion, he'd threatened the governor in the previous days and some thought he might try to assassinate him. A large-scale search was organized to find him. Instead of going after the governor, Corbett went to the home of a friend who'd been petitioning for his release from the asylum. The friend gave him money for train fare, which Corbett said he'd use to get to Mexico.

And that, believe it or not, is all we know.

Historically speaking, Corbett was never seen again. Despite urban legends, strange men crawling out of the woodwork claiming to be him, and partial clues about what ultimately happened to him (notably that he may have died in a tragic fire in Minnesota in 1894), there's no solid evidence that Corbett actually went to Mexico or anywhere else. He simply disappeared into history.

Say one thing for Boston Corbett—there's not much mystery about why he shot John Wilkes Booth. It was either self-defense or self-righteousness, nothing in between. The motivations of Corbett's counterpart, on the other hand, have always been clouded in confusion.

***

The odds of Jack Ruby having the opportunity to shoot Lee Harvey Oswald are right up there with winning the lottery or getting struck by lightning. Or maybe both at the same time.

Let's set the stage. It's Sunday morning, two days after the assassination. Oswald had been in police custody for 46 hours, questioned by essentially every branch of the government investigating the assassination: from the city and county police to the FBI to the Secret Service, even a U.S. postal inspector who was invited in for what would be the final interrogation session with Oswald that morning. In between, Oswald was paraded through the halls of the Dallas Police headquarters and answered further questions from reporters.

Procedurally, the time had come to transfer Oswald from the city jail to the county jail—the next routine step for anyone arrested for a major crime. Amid the swarm of confusion over that weekend, the Dallas Police had weighed several options for how and when to do this, from quietly and secretly moving him overnight to doing it in broad daylight in an armored car. Security was on their minds but not nearly enough (see earlier note about reporters being able to walk up to Oswald and ask random questions in the hallways). The decision was made to transfer him publicly to demonstrate to the world that he was being treated humanely. Another more PR-centered purpose was to stave off criticism from members of the media that the Dallas Police weren't being cooperative with them.

They decided to transfer Oswald around 10:00 on Sunday morning, and the reporters were informed of this so they could be there.

Jack Ruby was a puzzling character who stumbled into infamy by impulsively shooting Lee Harvey Oswald, thereby fueling conspiracy theories for years to come. He is shown here with his lawyer Sam H. Clinton (left). Journalist Robert Huffaker holds a microphone in his hand (Bill Winfrey Collection, The Dallas Morning News/The Sixth Floor Museum at Dealey Plaza).

Many were, even though it would be more than an hour past the announced time before the event would actually take place. By 11, the parking garage in the basement of the department—where Oswald would be escorted into the car that would take him across town— was filled with people who had been waiting and planning for this moment all night.

Jack Ruby wasn't one of them.

Ruby was the kind of guy who really didn't plan anything. He just sort of wandered through his days and nights with no real motivational or logical propulsion. Consequently, his shooting of Oswald was the equivalent of an impulse buy of a candy bar at a grocery store cash register. The great irony of it all is that had he actually planned to shoot Oswald that morning, his disorganization and lack of attention to detail likely would have prevented him from doing so.

This feels perversely appropriate, since Ruby was a living contradiction. He was obsessed with personal hygiene, often taking two or three showers a day ... but his apartment was a pigsty. He made his living selling alcohol and flaunting women ... but rarely drank or got involved with women himself. He was a fitness freak ... but had the physique of Barney Rubble. More than anything, he longed for respect and class ... yet immersed himself with the people and places that defined the greasy underbelly of Dallas society.

So, almost by accident, Ruby found himself at the centerpiece of one of the most stunning moments in history when he shot Oswald on a sudden and random impulse at 11:21 that Sunday morning. How can we conclude it was on impulse, you ask? Well, for starters, just four minutes before he pulled the trigger, Ruby was at a Western Union office sending a money order to a stripper. For most of us, that action alone would have made it a memorable day, but for Ruby it was business as usual, as he sauntered from one bizarre activity to the next.

In those four minutes, Jack Ruby transformed from a guy running errands on a Sunday morning to the most mysterious man in America. After sending the money order, he walked out of the Western Union and started down the Main Street sidewalk. About 100 yards down the street, he noticed a pack of people swarming around the entrance to the parking garage to Dallas Police headquarters. Anything surrounded by a swarm of curious bystanders was the kind of thing that attracted Ruby like a moth to a flame. As an experienced gate-crasher, he confidently and casually walked to the entrance, slipped through the narrow gap between the wall and the armored car that was parked there (a decoy for the car Oswald was actually being moved in), and walked down the ramp into the basement unnoticed.

At the bottom of the ramp, Ruby merged into the gaggle of reporters and cameramen who had waited hours for this moment. Ruby, conversely, stood there for roughly 60 seconds before Oswald was brought out. Then, seeing what he interpreted as a smug little smile on Oswald's face, Ruby snapped. Pulling out the .38 snub-nosed revolver he usually carried with him, Ruby lunged forward and shot Oswald in the stomach. All while more than 100 people—including better than 70 police officers—stood there and watched.

Oswald was rushed to Parkland Hospital, where he died less than two hours later. The madness of Friday's assassination had now been compounded by a second act of undefined and frightening violence, this one broadcast on live television to an already jittery nation. Thus launched a thousand questions, starting with the most obvious: Why? How? And first and foremost, *Who?*

Like Boston Corbett, Jack Ruby initially went by another name. Born Jacob Rubenstein, he grew up in the Jewish neighborhoods of Chicago, the son of Polish immigrants. He was a quick-tempered and disobedient child who watched his father frequently arrested for disorderly conduct and battery. Years later, he'd see his mother committed to a mental hospital. He managed to stay in school through eighth grade, but his real education took place on the streets. As he got older, he'd scalp tickets to sporting events and later tried his hand as an entrepreneur. He was involved in a chapter of Chicago's scrap iron and junk handlers union for a time, then after World War II, he moved to Dallas to help his sister Eva with her burgeoning restaurant and nightclub businesses. Upon arriving in Texas, he legally changed his last name to "Ruby." It was a curious and symbolic choice for a man so proud of being Jewish and so sensitive about insulting remarks made about Jews. But this was Texas, and he would have been an obviously Jewish businessman—in essence, creating the chocolate and peanut butter of intolerance.

The next fifteen years of Ruby's life sketched out like a Richter scale reading. He made fruitful connections and started several promising business ventures. Then he had a mental breakdown and, in his words, "hibernated" in a state of deep depression at a cheap motel for four months when those ventures went bad. He rebounded, eventually opening what would become his signature business: the Carousel Club, a grimy after-hours establishment that would become Ruby's entire world. He served as emcee and proprietor, booking strippers and luring in customers to see them. Often, he also served as bouncer, physically removing and getting into altercations with troublesome customers, or in some cases, his own employees. On one occasion, he got into a fight with one of the club's musicians, who bit off the tip of Ruby's left index finger in the scuffle.

A large portion of his clientele was made up of Dallas police officers, whom Ruby came to know well. He loved cops, even though his actions occasionally required their professional attention. Prior to his shooting Oswald, Ruby was arrested eight different times by the Dallas Police, for offenses ranging from violating city liquor ordinances to disturbing the peace to carrying a concealed weapon. Still, he never harbored any ill will toward Dallas's finest, and would often invite them to his nightclub or let them know about any shady dealings he heard about from some of his unsavory customers.

Reflected by his relationship with the police, Ruby always saw himself as something more than he actually was. While he certainly had some seedy acquaintances, he perpetually implied that he was kind of a big deal, even suggesting that he had underworld connections. If anything was going on anywhere around him, Ruby wanted to be a part of it, to be where the action was. And there had never been more action in Big D than the Kennedy assassination and its aftermath.

At the moment of the assassination, Ruby was at the offices of the *Dallas Morning News*, placing an ad for his nightclub. He found out what had happened within minutes, and the assassination immediately became the most important thing in his life. Over the next two days, he tried to emotionally recover from the blow. He'd occasionally burst into uncontrollable bouts of sobbing, telling anyone who would listen that this was the worst thing to ever happen to the city of Dallas. He cried harder about Kennedy's death, his friends and family would explain, than he did about the death of his own parents. He closed his nightclub for the entire weekend out of respect and raged over any other businesses that didn't.

Naturally, with the Dallas Police Department serving as the nexus of all of this following Oswald's arrest, Ruby couldn't help but insert himself into it. He wandered the hallways of police headquarters late into the night on Friday, carrying a notebook and deputizing himself as a reporter. Really, he acted more as a journalistic pimp, setting up interviews with Dallas officials for friends he had in the media. He even slipped into a late-night press conference in which Oswald formally spoke to reporters. He bought sandwiches for police and genuinely felt like he was a part of what was happening, all the while handing out free passes to his nightclub to out-of-town reporters covering the assassination.

By now, Jack Ruby is probably reminding you of someone. Most of us know (or have known) guys like this: a self-promoting dude-bro who always seems to be around, making himself an essential part of every story. Irritating, maybe, but otherwise harmless. So at what point did Jack Ruby decide to become a murderer?

The short answer is 11:21 Sunday morning. Ruby always said he never planned on shooting Oswald before he did it. And considering his random path—geographically and emotionally—to the basement of police headquarters, that totally checks out.

If you're looking for a motive for his impulse, there are two primary drivers. The first was his intense grief over the assassination, which was multi-layered and ratcheted up like a pressure cooker all weekend. In addition to the same shock and sorrow that so much of the nation felt, Ruby specifically hated how it had tainted his beloved hometown (the "City of Hate" roots just beginning to take hold). He also feared a roundabout backlash on Jews. The apparent motivation behind killing the president mirrored the spirit of an aggressively anti–Kennedy ad that had been placed in the newspaper Friday morning. The credit line was an organization led by a man with a Jewish last name, which also appeared in the ad. Ruby was enraged by it, before and especially after the assassination, and felt personal embarrassment that a fellow Jew could have so harshly criticized his beloved, now murdered president.

But the two details that pushed Ruby's grief and anger over the edge were sparked by Ruby's sympathy for Kennedy's immediate family. Among the onslaught of interviews he read, listened to, or participated in over the weekend, a question was raised to the Dallas district attorney, who would be prosecuting Oswald, whether Jackie Kennedy would need to testify at the trial. The answer was a vague "hopefully-not-but-maybe." The idea of Jackie being forced to return to the site of the tragedy and relive it all again for this sniveling little punk named Oswald made Ruby's blood boil.

Then, on Sunday morning, Ruby read a heartfelt letter published in the newspaper. Written to five-year-old Caroline Kennedy by a man who'd come out to see JFK in the motorcade, he explained to the daughter of the fallen president how much her father had meant and how sad the entire world was for losing him. The letter crushed Ruby, and may have been what ultimately disintegrated whatever restraint might have stopped him from reacting when he saw Oswald's smirky face.

Then we must combine these emotional Roman candles with a recent news story Ruby remembered. The year before, a man who'd killed an undercover Dallas police officer was ultimately released when the charges were dismissed for lack of evidence. In the back of Ruby's mind all weekend was the lingering fear that this might happen to Oswald. Had Oswald confessed to the crime in the two days of questioning, Ruby would explain, this fear would have been allayed and he never would have shot him.

All of these things were stewing in Ruby's scattered mind as he walked down the Main Street ramp into the basement on Sunday morning. When he saw Oswald's face, the pressure cooker exploded. "I hope I killed the son of a bitch!" Ruby cried as the police piled on top of him in the moments after the shooting. When one of the cops asked who they had at the bottom of the pile, Ruby replied, "Oh hell! You guys know me. I'm Jack Ruby."

As Oswald was rushed to Parkland Hospital, Ruby was peeled off the concrete floor and rushed into the elevator Oswald had just taken down to the basement. Along the way, Ruby began to explain his motivation. "Do you think I'm going to let the man who shot our president get away with it?" he said in the elevator, adding that killing Oswald "would save everybody a lot of trouble." When one of the officers commented that he thought Ruby had indeed killed Oswald, Ruby replied, "Somebody had to do it. You all couldn't." In Ruby's mind, much in the same way he'd deputized himself as a reporter, he also had made himself Oswald's judge, jury, and executioner.

"It was one chance in a million," he told the police as they reached the fifth-floor cell in which he would be held. "If I had planned this, I couldn't have had my timing any better."

Holy cow, was he right.

Consider the timeline. Two hours before shooting Oswald, Jack Ruby was still fast asleep after a late Saturday night. One hour before shooting Oswald, Ruby was sitting around his apartment in his underwear. Twenty minutes before shooting Oswald, Ruby still had yet to leave for the Western Union office. Five minutes before, he was down the street, filling out forms and standing in line.

The only reason he went out at all that morning was to send a money order to one of the strippers at his club who needed an advance to buy groceries. Since he'd closed the nightclub for the weekend, she was short on funds. So in the crucial moments just before Oswald was killed, his assassin was queued up at the Western Union office with his beloved dachshund sitting in his unlocked car parked on the street outside. It's also worth noting that Ruby loved that dachshund—Sheba, its name was—so much that he often referred to it as his wife. If he had any premeditated notion of shooting Oswald, he never would have brought the dog with him that morning and certainly wouldn't have left it alone in the car, not having any sense of when or even if he would be back.

Had the line at the Western Union been one person longer, had the police asked Oswald one less question, had Ruby stopped at his car before going down the ramp, had Oswald not asked to put on a sweater before the transfer ... you get the picture. Had a dozen different variables not clicked into place in the exact right order at the exact right time, Ruby never would have had the opportunity to make history.

Like Boston Corbett 98 years before, Ruby's feverish rationale never allowed for the possibility of getting into trouble for shooting the president's assassin. He genuinely thought he'd be given a pat on the back and released. Plus, there would be the added bonus of showing the world that a Jew could have guts—counteracting the hateful Kennedy ad placed in the paper on Friday morning. Not only was Ruby buddy-buddy with the police department, but he genuinely saw nothing wrong with what he'd done. When a friend came to visit him in jail in the days following, Ruby commented, "I got balls, ain't I, baby?" To which the friend replied, "Yeah, Jack, and they're going to hang you by them, too."

Ruby was quickly tried, convicted, and sentenced to death the following March. As he wallowed in prison, Ruby's loose grip on reality began to slip. He told visitors he could hear screaming in the walls, which he attributed to Jews being boiled in oil and slaughtered in the basement of the jail (eerily similar to Major Henry Rathbone's nightmarish visions inside a German asylum a half-century earlier). Ruby made several attempts to kill himself: electrocution, hanging, and the less-efficient tactic of running headfirst into a concrete wall (another callback, this one to suicide plays attempted by some of Booth's co-conspirators in prison).

Two years later, the court of appeals overturned Ruby's conviction and sentence based on the determination that Ruby couldn't have been provided a fair trial in Dallas. A retrial was ordered to be held in Wichita Falls, but when deputies arrived to transfer Ruby, he was too ill to travel. Initially diagnosed with pneumonia, Ruby actually had advanced cancer, which had spread to his liver, brain, and lungs. He died a few days later, officially of a blood clot, thus closing the book on one of the most enigmatic characters in American history.

Obviously, Ruby's tale has always and will always fan the flames of conspiracy theories. Most paint Ruby as a mob enforcer who silenced Oswald for the mafia, which had orchestrated a hit on the president. Then Ruby himself was taken out of the picture before he could confess what he knew. Most conspiracy buffs saw Jack Ruby as a tragically intriguing character, something out of a movie. So naturally, he was eventually made *into* a movie.

Cranked out in the afterglow of Oliver Stone's phantasmagorical *JFK* in 1992, *Ruby* drafts off many of the same alternative assassination theories. Versatile actor Danny Aiello portrays Ruby less as an addlebrained charlatan than as a lovable palooka with fringe mob ties (picture Uncle Buck as a Corleone). Picking up a few threads of reality and weaving them into a thick wool sweater of historical inaccuracy, the film follows Ruby as he walks the tightrope of casual mob assassin and reluctant CIA informant. Along the way he encounters actual historical figures so thinly veiled as fictional characters it's both comical and not worth the effort. The upshot of the film is that, of course, the mob killed Kennedy. More interestingly, it hedges its bet by positing that Jack Ruby wasn't *ordered* to silence Oswald as much as he simply saw it as his job to do so and took the initiative—like a cat dropping a dead mouse at your front door. The *New York Times* called it "rudely entertaining"—which is at least half right—but not surprisingly, it was a commercial flop. (And yet now totally worth watching for then-unknown David Duchovny's blink-and-you-miss-it performance as Southern-drawling Dallas police officer J.D. Tippit.)

As evidenced by his cinematic portrayal, the problems with the baseline theory of Jack Ruby as a mob enforcer are legion. At the most basic level, they boil down to the timing elements. If Oswald were to be silenced before he could turn on his benefactors, the optimal time to do so would have been *before* he was questioned by police for 46 hours, not after. Likewise, were Ruby a mob button man, it was probably not ideal to provide him with two-and-a-half years to tell his story to anyone who would listen before casually putting him in the ground as an afterthought.

More than that, though, the reason why the conspiracy theories flame out almost instantly is Jack Ruby himself. From everything we know about him, he's basically the last guy on the planet you'd want involved with your super-secret, high-stakes murder/cover-up bacchanal.

Ruby was, in the words of a reporter who knew him well, "the quintessential wanna-be but never was." Had he been approached to participate in the assassination cover-up in any way, there's absolutely no chance he would have or could have kept that a secret. He would have told somebody, if not *everybody*. Ruby was clearly not someone you could count on for something as cosmically important as this. This was reflected by his shooting Oswald not in the head or heart, but in the abdomen—a wound that Oswald had a decent chance of surviving. Had Ruby indeed been assigned to kill Oswald, even the most incompetent mafioso would face-palm at Ruby's shoddy technique. And whoever decided Ruby was the right guy to go to for this would very quickly be sleeping with the fishes.

Whether or not Ruby was ordered to take out Oswald, consider the path not taken. If Ruby didn't belly-flop himself into history, Oswald would have been transferred to the county jail, stood trial, been found guilty, and—here's the funny part—most of the conspiracy theories dreamed up since would never have taken root. Rather than shutting down the suspicion of conspiracy (as the conspiracy theorists claim Ruby was doing by silencing Oswald), Ruby's action kept it alive for all time. If he was indeed part of the cover-up and this was the ultimate result ... ladies and gentlemen, we've discovered the most epic fail in American history.

Even without the intrigue of conspiracy, Jack Ruby remains a question mark. Throughout his life, logic rarely broke the skin of anything he did. He lived along his own strange dark country road— where, after the assassination, the scarecrows came to life.

In the Yiddish spoken by his ancestors, Ruby was a *meshuga*. From the Hebrew root "meshuge," which translates back to the word we started with: "crazy."

A tough word to define. Just like the assassins' assassins.

12

So What?

Piece by piece, we've broken down that original list of creepy coincidences put together by Dr. Matrix, marketed by the Historical Documents Company, and recognized around the world. We've traced the winding path of artifacts, looked at potential curses, explored beloved historic sites and museums, and become acquainted with the cast of characters that all connect the assassinations to one another. Hopefully you've had some fun and maybe even learned some things along the way.

But as we near the end of our journey, there's one question left. A question you may have been asking all along.

So what?

Why does any of this matter and what does any of it mean? What, if anything, are we supposed to do with this information?

If you made it this far, it's a fair question.

The safe answer, the one that most serious historians can get on board with, is actually quite simple.

Absolutely nothing.

Many would conclude that the long list of curious coincidences is fun, but nothing more. At best, it's a blip on the radar scope of history. At worst, it's a Ouija board planchette operated by twitchy fingers. Some look at this list as evidence supporting the grumpy old saw about coincidence: if 10,000 monkeys banged away on typewriters for 10,000 years, sooner or later they would reproduce the complete works of Shakespeare. In other words, if you look hard enough and long enough at anything, patterns will inevitably emerge.

Odds are, that's closer to correct than where we're about to go.

But just for a moment, let's consider the alternative. And in order to do that, we must open our minds a bit. Because any other answer to "So what?" is going to require that.

What if, by putting all of these coincidences together, each ceases to be a coincidence? What if they're ... pick the term you're comfortable with ... something else?

A term some would choose is "synchronicity." Not the Police's final and most successful studio album, but the coincidental occurrence of events (especially psychic events) that seem related but are not explained by conventional mechanisms of causality. The concept was first introduced in the 1950s by Swiss psychologist Carl Jung, who believed in a collective unconscious that connects all mankind in ways we don't understand. Put simply, synchronicity is meaningful coincidence that can provide guidance—as if the universe is winking at you. Without a doubt, synchronicity is determined by the user. What one reads into a coincidence is always open to interpretation, and clearly, not all coincidences are evidence of synchronicity. The real question is, are any?

For those who accept it (even if they don't understand it), synchronicity can have practical applications. In addition to providing meaning and comfort in a world of chaos, it's like finding little invisible post-it notes that tell you you're on the right path in your journey. Or can nudge you toward making a certain decision. Or maybe even tell you when something's about to happen.

For instance, one synchronic theory is that we could have—hypothetically, of course—predicted Kennedy's assassination based on the connective tissue to Lincoln's assassination. Which isn't to cast blame on anyone via metaphysical Monday-morning quarterbacking or even infer that we actually should have correctly forecasted anything. Hopefully we can all agree that this type of thinking really shouldn't be a part of the Secret Service's objective.

That being said, let's kick around that idea for a minute. If you find any credibility in the prediction theory, then is it not possible that a string of coincidences like this could happen again? And that maybe—just maybe—we could recognize a connection between a future president and a past one? By which we could be aware of the possibility of a tragic event and be on the lookout for it? Something akin to a tornado watch—a funnel cloud hasn't been spotted, but the conditions are right for it.

It sounds crazy, and probably is. And yet, awfully alluring.

How great would it be if the universe (or fate or destiny, however you want to label it) could communicate to us? What if something cosmically powerful was trying to help us out, to provide us with next-level insight about either our past or our future. Or maybe even both.

Looking at it another way, instead of a communication, what if it's evidence of a multiverse or alternate dimension? And this list of curious coincidences represents some sort of fissure between that world and ours.

Admittedly, we're getting weird now. Which makes it a great time to talk about the Berenstain Bears.

In recent years, an urban legend circulated across the internet (where else) centered on an alarming number of people who *swear* that the name of the beloved cartoon family of biped bears is "BerenstEIn," spelled with an "e-i." It's actually "BerenstAIn," though people will passionately argue that they remember it being spelled the other way when they were kids. (Stop and think about it—which do you remember?)

This story led to potential explanations, with the most fun based on a time traveler being sent back to stop a Y2K catastrophe, then somehow causing a ripple effect that's reflected by the different spelling. Another (more believable?) theory explains that the people who know it as "Berenstain" are from one dimension, and the "Berenstein" folks at some point crossed over from a parallel universe into this one. When that happened exactly is unclear, but evidently sometime after the Berenstain Bears entered the cultural zeitgeist.

Technically, this is called the "Mandela Effect." The label refers to the more substantial example of the number of people who were convinced that Nelson Mandela died in prison in 1985. In reality (the current reality, if you like), Mandela was released from prison in 1990, served five years as South African president, and then died in

2013. And yet there are people who vividly remember watching his funeral on television 28 years earlier.

Those who believe in this call these conflicting memories "residue"—like tiny fragments rubbed off a multi-dimensional pencil eraser that wiped away a timeline which was then replaced by another. Could the Lincoln and Kennedy similarities be an example of a comparable kind of residue?

Whether it's a warning system or evidence of alternate realities, let's consider the possibilities. What if, for the sake of argument, a future president has the same number of letters in their name as William McKinley or James Garfield? Or has a vice president with the same name as McKinley's or Garfield's? Or, taking it out of the assassination realm, has similar connections with any of the other four presidents who died due to health reasons while in office?

Remember, we actually have seen this idea dip its toe into the water. Back in 1959, someone wrote a letter to JFK clueing him in on the 20-year presidential curse. The next time around, it actually came up as a question to one of the candidates during the 1980 campaign. And this had to—if only briefly—be on some people's minds in the frantic hours of March 30, 1981, following the shooting of Ronald Reagan. Not only because of the reemergence of the possibility of the 20-year Curse of Tippecanoe, but also an examination of the similarities between Reagan's potential assassination and James Garfield's.

A ricocheted bullet struck the 70-year-old Reagan beneath his left arm, fractured a rib, punctured his lung, and caused serious internal bleeding. He was near death by the time he reached George Washington University Hospital but was stabilized and underwent emergency surgery to correct the wounds. He spent the next 11 days in the hospital before being released.

Thanks to the quick and successful work of Reagan's security detail and the medical teams that treated him, we never needed to connect dots to a new assassination. We never needed to note that Ronald Reagan and James Garfield were both elected president 100 years apart—Garfield the twentieth president, Reagan the fortieth. Or that they were both shot in Washington, D.C., at locations less than three miles apart. Or that they had the same number of letters in their names. And so on.

Another detail worth noting is the similarity in their wounds and the vast differences in the type of medical care they received. Reagan's wound was actually much more serious, but he received world-class treatment immediately and quickly recovered. By contrast, Garfield was taken through a series of questionable medical decisions over the next several months that actually turned out to cause more damage than the shooting. Most notably, his doctors repeatedly rooted around inside Garfield's chest for the bullet with their bare hands and unsterilized medical tools, which led to widespread infection.

Once Reagan survived his shooting—and then his remaining eight years as president—there was no reason for the comparisons to Garfield to be made. It became a moot point. Yet most people don't realize how frighteningly close Reagan came to dying that day. Or what impact that might have had on the veracity of these connections. (Here again, if you buy into the altered timeline theory—Reagan surviving could be construed as an abrupt rewrite when many other indicators pointed toward his demise.)

So maybe that's where it all ended. Maybe Reagan's survival broke both the potential 20-year presidential curse cycle and any kind of metaphysical warning system that may have existed. Or, looking at it another way, maybe it was Nancy Reagan who actually snapped the cosmos's streak. Perhaps it was her interest and attention to astrology, as it related to her husband's safety, that turned everything around. All of which was prompted by the assassination attempt and March 30 being a "bad" day for Reagan. Had she not taken such a unique and active interest in that realm, perhaps something else might have happened to Reagan later in his tenure as president. In her own words: "Was the shooting in March 1981 merely an omen, an early warning that something even worse might lie ahead?"

In fact, astrology is another possible explanation for the coincidences. Specifically, a conjunction between Jupiter and Saturn, which happens every 20 years ... and aligns exactly with the Curse of Tippecanoe. This has led to countless astrologers putting together and comparing charts and signs for various presidents to find clarity and connection.

Astrology aside, if the Reagans didn't end the string (i.e., if his getting shot "counts"), then George W. Bush certainly did. First elected in 2000, Bush also survived his presidency, with no serious close calls. There was an incident in which a live grenade was thrown in the general vicinity of Bush during a speech in the nation of Georgia in 2005, but the grenade didn't detonate. Even if it had, it likely wouldn't have posed any real threat to the president's life.

Some consider that on par with Reagan surviving his assassination attempt, mostly as part of an effort to keep the streak alive. By that line of thinking, the 20-year cycle and/or warning signs are connected to the assassination attempts/near-brushes with death and not to the presidents themselves. In which case, perhaps Reagan's shooting and Bush's grenade dodge prove that the curse still exists—they merely sidestepped it.

Here's yet another way to look at it. What if the connection is limited just to Lincoln and Kennedy? Thus, rather than projecting it forward as a warning system, what if instead it reflects a backward look? By that rationale, perhaps these coincidences aren't haunting or malicious, but poetic and philosophical. Here were two charismatic, smart guys who would come to embody and define so much of what an American president could and should be. What if these coincidences are some sort of cosmic wink, a multidimensional sign of respect?

Or, some would argue, a sign of reincarnation.

Before you chuckle at the idea, it's important to understand what that means, especially since it's a bit of a fringe belief in western culture. In the cinematic terms we tend to lean toward to help us process supernatural possibilities, reincarnation is not a *Freaky Friday* switcheroo—as if Abraham Lincoln wound up in Kennedy's body—nor a *Groundhog Day* scenario in which Lincoln is repeatedly reliving the same fate. It's a religious and philosophical belief, most commonly accepted in Asia, that a soul is reborn in another living thing after death. If you do need a movie to anchor to, think *A Dog's Purpose*: the same furry, lovable soul placed into different canines over several decades, eventually winding up back with its original owner four dogs later. Silly and schmaltzy as it may sound, it was a setup enticing enough to gross $200 million worldwide at the box office. However you feel about it, the reincarnation theory appears to have legs. Four of them, at least.

A common thread through the belief in reincarnation is the cause-and-effect principle of karma: what you do in your present life will have an impact on your next. In some interpretations, the reincarnated face the same situations in different lives as a way to learn from them. Put another way, in a callback to the lyrics of Buddy Starcher's hit record in the 1960s, history tends to repeat itself.

The bottom line is that none of us knows for sure what happens after a person dies. There are a multitude of theories, and reincarnation is one of them. Unfortunately, there's a tendency to see any beliefs about life and death other than yours as completely nuts. So to dismiss someone's belief in reincarnation as nonsense but embrace the idea of heaven would be, by definition, hypocritical. Maybe neither is right. Or maybe both are.

When you put reincarnation in its proper context and remove some of our pop culture shortcuts, who's to say it doesn't apply in this case. Maybe John Kennedy was a reincarnated Abraham Lincoln, ultimately doomed to the same fate. And all of the coincidences connecting them came to light only because of their historical importance and the widely researched nature of their deaths. Maybe any or all instances of reincarnation have a similar ripple effect—we just never were compelled to look for reasons to connect a fisherman from Japan to an insurance agent from Iowa who lived and died 200 years apart.

Then there's the more familiar branch of the life-after-death tree: ghosts.

Over the past century-plus, there have been numerous people who have claimed to see the ghost of Abraham Lincoln in the White House. Not tourists or ghost hunters, mind you, but members of the White House staff, guests, even first ladies and presidents themselves. Calvin Coolidge's wife Grace said she saw Lincoln's ghost in the Oval Office, gazing out the window at the Potomac River. In the

1930s, the visiting Queen of the Netherlands heard a knock at her bedroom door in the middle of the night. Opening it, she saw Lincoln standing there. Dwight Eisenhower claimed to have seen Lincoln walking down a White House hallway, and Eleanor Roosevelt, who used the Lincoln bedroom as an office, reported occasionally feeling his presence. Winston Churchill told a story of seeing and even speaking to Lincoln's ghost in his White House bedroom during a visit in the 1940s.

Lincoln is just one of several reported ghost sightings in the White House, but he seems to be the most predominant. "They say Lincoln always comes back whenever he feels the country is in need or in peril," James Broach, who operates haunted tours around the country, told the *Washington Post* in 2017. "They say he just strides up and down the second-floor hallways and raps on doors and stands by windows."

Adding even more intrigue to these tales is the interest Lincoln had in supernatural elements—primarily the significance of dreams and omens.

Reportedly, Lincoln told a friend of a dream he'd had just a few months before the assassination. "There seemed to be a deathlike stillness about me," he described. "Then I heard subdued sobs, as if a number of people were weeping. I thought I left my bed and wandered downstairs.... I arrived at the East Room. Before me was a catafalque, on which rested a corpse wrapped in funeral vestments. Around it were stationed soldiers who were acting as guards; and there was a throng of people, some gazing mournfully upon the corpse, whose face was covered, others weeping pitifully. 'Who is dead in the White House?' I demanded of one of the soldiers. 'The President,' was his answer. 'He was killed by an assassin.'"

Some historians dismiss the story as fabricated for entertainment purposes long after Lincoln's death. But if true, there's no other way to describe it than as a premonition, and an eerily accurate one.

Keep in mind that John Kennedy's funeral and all the pomp and circumstance leading up to it was deliberately designed to mimic Lincoln's—from the funeral procession through the streets of Washington to a public display in the rotunda in the Capitol Building.

Both coffins even lay in state on the same spot in the East Room of the White House.

So is it possible that Lincoln wasn't seeing a premonition of *his* death, but of John Kennedy's? (Let *that* idea melt your brain for a second.)

Even if you dismiss that dream, there are other, less on-the-nose visions Lincoln experienced that are more generally accepted as fact. The best example was a dream he'd had just after being elected in 1860 in which he saw two images of his own face in a mirror—one very clear and the other blurry. Mary Lincoln interpreted the faces as representations of Lincoln's tenure as president: the clear image of his face indicated he'd survive his first term, but the more ghostlike reflection suggested he wouldn't make it through his second.

Really, it was Mary's belief in the supernatural that sparked Lincoln's own fascination in the subject. Much of Mary's interest was driven by the grief of losing two young sons, the second tragedy occurring while the Lincolns were in the White House when 11-year-old Willie died of typhoid fever. Mary held seances at the White House in an attempt to contact them, and we know that Lincoln attended at least a couple. Lincoln himself spoke of receiving spectral visits from Willie in the White House.

It's tempting to try to tie together Lincoln's supernatural leanings (both before and after death) to the assassination connection list. Maybe that's what kicked over the first domino—Lincoln either believing in or perhaps even unconsciously creating some sort of ghostly echo through the magnitude and tragic nature of his death. After all, that seems to be the key ingredient of most ghost stories.

Conversely, there are no reports of anyone seeing John Kennedy's ghost (or, for that matter, of Kennedy seeing anyone else's), which seems to make sense. While Lincoln's persona lends itself to gothic mysticism, JFK's just seems too cool for such an enterprise. Much in the same way you don't hear stories about the ghost of Frank Sinatra.

Ghosts, reincarnation, a tear in the fabric of our dimension, or a tap on the shoulder from the cosmos—maybe there's something to one or more of them. Maybe it's all nonsense. Either way, there's just no way to know.

Consequently, maybe that's the answer to the initial question. If the question is "So what?" then perhaps the answer is "Why not?"

Most of us do tend to believe in a little "why not" from time to time. Little moments you experience or hear of that make no sense at all and seem incalculably random. On the anniversary of a loved one's death, you see her name on a passing car's license plate. Thinking about an old friend you haven't talked to in years right before they call you on the phone. You feel like you're being steered a certain way when making a big decision but can't quite figure out why or where it's coming from.

If you believe those kinds of things can happen, is it that crazy to subscribe substance to the Lincoln-Kennedy coincidences? For what it's worth, history is littered with little moments exactly like these.

John Adams and Thomas Jefferson, a pair of our Founding Fathers who'd worked together to create the Declaration of Independence, both died within hours of one another on the fiftieth anniversary of its signing—July 4, 1826.

Mark Twain, arguably America's greatest writer, was born just as Halley's Comet appeared in 1835, then died the day after it reemerged following its 75-year cycle in 1910.

In 1861, Wilmer McLean, a farmer in Manassas, Virginia, had his home commandeered by Confederate officers and used as their headquarters for the Battle of Bull Run—the first battle of the Civil War. Shortly after, seeking a simpler life away from the conflict, McLean moved his family to the quiet town of Appomattox Court House, about 120 miles away. It was in McLean's new home, in April 1865, that General Robert E. Lee surrendered to Ulysses S. Grant, bringing the four-year struggle to a close. The Civil War had literally begun in McLean's front yard and ended in his front parlor.

And let's not leave out one of the spookiest examples of all, which ties directly back to Lincoln's assassination. In late 1864, just a few months before his father would be shot, Robert Todd Lincoln was traveling by train to Washington. As he was waiting at a stop in Jersey City, he stepped back on the train platform to let others pass and leaned against a stopped train. When that train suddenly began to move, Robert lost his balance and would have fallen into the gap between the moving train and the platform, which would have seriously injured or even killed him. He was saved when a quick-thinking bystander grabbed him by the collar and pulled him back onto the platform. That bystander was Edwin Booth—John Wilkes Booth's older brother—who was traveling to Richmond, Virginia, ... with John Ford, owner of Ford's Theatre.

So these things do happen.

Ultimately it comes down to a basic question: is it better that all of this means something or that it doesn't? Are we more comfortable with the idea that the long list of coincidences is entirely random or that it's evidence of a deeper significance? Or, looking at it another way, is one line of thinking scarier than the other?

To be fair, it's also possible to read too much into the connections. Harvard University's humor publication *Demon Magazine* put together its own parody version of the list, which noted that both Lincoln and Kennedy were succeeded by their vice presidents, and that both men (except Kennedy) were born in log houses. Another gem: Lincoln's wife's maiden name was "Todd," which (ignoring one of the d's) read backwards, is "dot," one of the two symbols used in Morse code, created by Samuel Morse, who invented the telegraph in 1844. Kennedy's wife Jackie later married Aristotle Onassis, from Greece, which had a civil war in 1944, exactly 100 years later. The satirical website ClickHole offered its own list, including the revelation that both Lincoln and Kennedy had vice presidents, wives, sons, and Labradors named Johnson.

No doubt about it, there's fun to be had with extraneous enthusiasm for the topic. Which is a nice counterbalance for conversations about life after death and alternate universes and time travel that also stem off this topic.

Which, once again, cycles us back to the original question: So what?

Fittingly, we wind up back where we started—to Martin Gardner (aka Dr. Matrix), the creator of the original list. Gardner himself represents the two sides of this question. His entire opus was rooted in math and science, celebrating their rock-solid certainty and debunking fringe elements that cheapened both. And yet, his love for wonder and whimsy was strong enough to recognize these coincidences and string them all together.

We saw the two viewpoints on this topic perfectly reflected earlier. One side from the father and one from his son. Jim Gardner offered the ying: "It's in our nature to find some sort of order to it that may not be there," while Martin Gardner offered the yang: "Every pattern of symbols conceals a secret meaning, though it may require great skill to discover it."

At the end of the day, maybe it's a tail-chasing exercise. We'll almost certainly never know for sure, and maybe that's for the best. We can leave this list of curious coincidences right where it is, as history's ultimate Rorschach test. Much in the same way we can look up at the sky on a summer afternoon and see large, fluffy clouds. Some of us see shapes, symbols, and sequence, while some of us don't. None of us is wrong. Though we can all agree that there are definitely clouds.

The first cloud was a random suggestion for Lincoln's running mate two years before he ran for president, a name that wouldn't have any real significance for 100 years.

More clouds would float across the sky in the decades to come. The potential curse which haunted our chief executives for over a century. The implausibly identical destinies of the artifacts which figuratively and literally carried the stains of tragedy. The troubling stories of the star-crossed bystanders as well as the assassins' assassins. The fall and rise of the brick-and-mortar representations of America's most infamous murders.

Coincidences all, which reside beneath the umbrella of the question mark that appears on the poster that spotlights the topic. The poster that has sparked the attention and imagination of young visitors to museum gift shops for years and likely will continue to for many more, defined by a cryptic headline in bold, black type.

"Lincoln-Kennedy Coincidence?"

Not a declaration, but a possibility. Not a statement, but a question.

One that each of us can answer for ourselves in the same way we can decide what we see when we look up at the sky. You may visualize figures and patterns floating high above us or simply see large puffs of water vapor that represent nothing at all.

The important thing is to never stop looking.

Acknowledgments

The evolution of this book, in one form or another, took nearly 20 years. And for much of that period, it looked like it would never materialize. So I'd be remiss not to acknowledge those who helped drag it (and me) across the finish line.

I have to thank editor Gary Mitchem for believing in this, and everyone at McFarland & Company who helped turn it into reality. Likewise, I must offer my gratitude to everyone I interviewed for the book, many of whom offered their time while juggling other responsibilities in the midst of a global pandemic: Matt Anderson, David Byers, Stephen Fagin, April Foran, Jim Gardner, Harry Rubenstein, Charles Sable, and Alan Weiss.

Much changed in the years I spent crafting this book, but one constant was my two fine sons, Jacob and Zachary, for whom my heart bursts with love and pride. I thank them for being exactly who they are and going along with me on several of the journeys that worked their way into this book. (And even for counting our steps as we strolled across the Henry Ford Museum on a summer afternoon.)

I also offer eternal gratitude to my parents, for putting up with me on the family vacations when I first became ensorcelled with these topics, and my sister Jeannine for hanging out with me in all those museum gift shops—usually scouting out the candy selection while I was screwing around with the poster rack.

I have to thank Jessica and Annabelle for their guidance and expertise on the statistical nature of permutations (and life in general, I suppose). And, just as importantly, Evan for his low-key sense of humor and for generally being a voice of reason. I also have to acknowledge the noble Bear for lying loyally by my side as I added the finishing touches, and Nala for providing the soundtrack while I did.

And of course, where would I be without the incredible and incomparable Julie Jeanne Pugh and her encouragement, advice, and support in this endeavor and so many others. She has made this (and me) so much better, and for that reason—and countless more—she has captured my heart.

Finally, while there are many of us who have a fascination with assassination, it's important not to lose sight of and always remember the two human beings we lost on those terrible days. It's easy to romanticize Abraham Lincoln and John Kennedy and overlook their flaws. But there's a reason for that. They were compassionate men, strong leaders, and, in the final analysis, great presidents who deserved so much better from the people they served.

In that spirit, we continually reflect upon their tragic conclusions and carry on in the eternal hope that learning about their legacies might help us become the people they inspired us to be.

Sources

Prologue: Running Mates

The description of Israel Green's letter and suggestion of John Kennedy as Abraham Lincoln's running mate comes from *The Magic Numbers of Dr. Matrix* by Martin Gardner (Prometheus Books, 1985) and the March 1893 issue of the *Magazine of American History* as well as the *Cincinnati Daily Gazette* and the *Findlay Morning Republican*.

Chapter 1

The background of the Historical Documents Company comes from its website (histdocs.com) as well as an interview with Alan Weiss. Throughout the book, details about the assassinations and many of the people involved were drawn from several sources: *The Day Kennedy Was Shot* by Jim Bishop (HarperCollins, 1968); *The Day Lincoln Was Shot* by Jim Bishop (Gramercy Books, 1955); *Backstage at the Lincoln Assassination* by Thomas A. Bogart (Regnery History, 2013); *Reclaiming History: The Assassination of John F. Kennedy* by Vincent Bugliosi (W.W. Norton & Co., 2007); *Kennedy and Lincoln: Medical & Ballistic Comparisons of Their Assassinations* by Dr. John Lattimer (Harcourt Brace, Jovanovich, 1980); *Case Closed: Lee Harvey Oswald and the Assassination of JFK* by Gerald Posner (Anchor Books, 1993); *Blood on the Moon: The Assassination of Abraham Lincoln* by Edward Steers, Jr. (University Press of Kentucky, 2001); *Bloody Crimes: The Funeral of Abraham Lincoln and the Chase for Jefferson Davis* by James Swanson (Harper Perennial, 2010); *End of Days: The Assassination of John F. Kennedy* by James Swanson (William Morrow, 2013); *Manhunt: The 12-Day Chase for Lincoln's Killer* by James Swanson (Harper Perennial, 2006); *President Kennedy Has Been Shot* by The Newseum with Cathy Trust and Susan Bennett (Sourcebooks Media Fusion, 2003); and *The Official Warren Commission Report on the Assassination of President John F. Kennedy* (Doubleday, 1964).

Chapter 2

The origin stories of both Dr. Matrix and Martin Gardner come from an interview with Jim Gardner as well as from Martin Gardner's books *The Magic Numbers of Dr. Matrix* (Prometheus Books, 1985) and *Undiluted Hocus-Pocus: The Autobiography of Martin Gardner* (Princeton University Press, 2013). Additional details were gleaned from an October 21, 2014, article on bbc.com ("Martin Gardner, Puzzle Master Extraordinaire"), martin-gardner.org, scientificamerican.com, and his obituary in the *Los Angeles Times,* with research about the spread of the original list of coincidences from *Time* and *Newsweek,* and details about Buddy Starcher's adaptation of the list from wfmu.org.

Chapter 3

Details for the "curse" were culled from a 2016 presentation by Marc Newman (Lifelong Learning Society instructor, Florida Atlantic University) accessed from c-span.org, in addition to thoughtco. com, indianapublicmedia.org, boston.com, snopes.com, and nytimes.com. Details about Tecumseh and Tenskwatawa and their conflicts with William Henry Harrison were drawn from *The Gods of Prophetstown: The Battle of Tippecanoe and the Holy War for the American Frontier* by Adam Jortner (Oxford University Press, 2012); *William Henry Harrison* by Gail Collins (Henry Holt, 2012); *A Sorrow in Our Heart: The Life of Tecumseh* by Allan W. Eckert (Bantam Books, 1992); *Tecumseh! A Play* by Allan W. Eckert (Little, Brown, 1974); and *Tecumseh: A Life* by John Sugden (Henry Holt, 1997). Other sources for details about the curse were drawn from an article in the November/December 2019 issue of *Skeptical Inquirer* ("The Presidential Curse and the Election of 2020" by Timothy Redmond), ohiohistorycentral.org, history.com, and nps.gov. Connected details about the potential assassination attempts of Jimmy Carter and Ronald Reagan were drawn from the *Dayton Daily News* and *My Turn: The Memoirs of Nancy Reagan* by Nancy Reagan with William Novak (Random House, 1989) as well as historyonthenet.com.

Chapter 4

The descriptions of detective John Kennedy's involvement in saving Lincoln on his way to Washington were drawn from *The Hour of Peril: The Secret Plot to Murder Lincoln Before the Civil War* by Daniel Stashower (Minotaur Books, 2013); *Blood on the Moon: The Assassination of Abraham Lincoln* by Edward Steers, Jr. (University Press of Kentucky, 2001); and Stashower's article "The Unsuccessful Plot to Kill Abraham Lincoln" from the February 2013 issue of *Smithsonian Magazine*. Descriptions and analysis of *The Tall Target* were culled from a March 6, 2012, article in *The New Yorker* ("DVD of the Week: The Tall Target" by Richard Brody), a March 2009 article in *America's Civil War Magazine*, archived at historynet.com ("ACW Review: The Tall Target" by Gordon Berg), and imdb.com.

Chapter 5

The accounts of the Lincoln rocker and the Kennedy limousine's paths to the Henry Ford Museum were drawn from interviews with Matt Anderson, Charles Sable, and Harry Rubenstein as well as the Henry Ford Museum website (thehenryford.com), oldcarsweekly.com, mlive.com, fox2detroit.com, abrahamlincolnonline.com, businessinsider.com, houstonpress.com, nydailynews.com, weta.org, usatoday.com, and an article in the January 1993 issue of *Popular Mechanics* ("Cars of the Presidents" by David W. Freeman). Details about the Henry Ford Museum and Dearborn were culled from thedailybeast.com, thenationalnews.com, and washingtonpost.com.

Chapter 6

The accounts of the background, assassination experiences, and ultimate fates of Henry Rathbone and Clara Harris were drawn from *Worst Seat in the House: Henry Rathbone's Front Row View of the Lincoln Assassination* by Caleb Jenner Stephens (Willow Manor Publishing, 2014), and the February/March 1994 issue of *American Heritage* ("The Haunted Major" by Gene Smith) as well as chicagotribune.com. Thematic interpretations of the relationship between Rathbone and Clara Harris were referenced from the novel *Henry and Clara* by Thomas Mallon (Vintage Books, 1994) and details about Clara Harris's "haunted dress" were drawn from *Things That Go Bump in the Night* by Louis Clark Jones (Syracuse University Press, 1983). The background and experiences for John Connally were drawn from *In History's Shadow: An American Odyssey* by John Connally with Mickey Herskowitz (Hyperion, 1993); *The Lone Star: The Life of John Connally* by James Reston, Jr. (Harper & Row, 1989); and his obituary in the *New York Times* and the November 2003 issue of *Texas Monthly* ("The Witness" by Mimi Swartz), along with upi.com, washingtonpost.com, and tsl.texas.gov.

Chapter 7

The details of the origin and history of Ford's Theatre were drawn from an interview with David Byers as well as *Images of America: Ford's Theatre* by Brian Anderson for the Ford's Theatre Society (Arcadia Publishing, 2014); *Backstage at the Lincoln Assassination* by Thomas A. Bogart (Regnery History, 2013); the Ford's Theatre website (fords.org), and newspapers.com as well as an April 14, 2015, article by Stephen J. Taylor for the Hoosier State Chronicles—Indiana's Digital Historic Newspaper Program (blog.newspapers.library.in.gov). Details of the *Marble Heart* story were drawn from these sources as well as a November 14, 2013, article by Al Hunter in *The Weekly View*. The origin and history of the Texas School Book Depository were drawn from an interview with Stephen Fagin as well as *Images of America: John F. Kennedy Sites in Dallas-Fort Worth* by Mark Doty and John H. Slate (Arcadia Publishing, 2013); *Assassination and Commemoration: JFK, Dallas, and the Sixth Floor Museum at Dealey Plaza* by Stephen Fagin (University of Oklahoma Press,

2013); *Images of America: Dealey Plaza* by John Slate and Willis C. Winters (Arcadia Publishing, 2013); the Sixth Floor Museum's website (jfk.org), and a November 21, 2013, article in *Smithsonian Magazine* ("The Architectural History of the JFK Assassination Site" by Jimmy Stamp), the *Rock Island Dispatch-Argus*, and the Texas State Historical Association Handbook of Texas (tshaonline.org). Details of the story of the sixth floor window were drawn from the *Dallas News* and *Dallas Observer*.

Chapter 8

Insight and analysis for the movies described were drawn from nytimes.com, tcm.com, rogerebert.com, history.com, jfk.hood.edu, smithsonianmag.com, washingtonpost.com, spaghetti-western.net, the Library of Congress website (loc.gov), and youtube.com.

Chapter 9

The details of the origin and history of the Petersen House and Osborn Oldroyd were drawn from an interview with David Byers as well as *Images of America: Ford's Theatre* by Brian Anderson for the Ford's Theatre Society (Arcadia Publishing, 2014), the Ford's Theatre website (fords.org), lincolnconspirators.com, lincolncollection.tumblr.com, and sangamoncountyhistory.org. Details for Parkland Hospital were drawn from an interview with April Foran as well as *Images of America: Parkland Hospital* by John W. Boyd, M.D. (Arcadia Publishing, 2015), the Parkland Hospital website (parklandhospital.com), and the hospital newsletter *Highlights*. The details about the transfer of Trauma Room 1 artifacts are drawn from the above as well as the *Twin Cities Pioneer Press* (twincities.com) and a January 28, 2008, article in the *Kansas City Star*.

Chapter 10

The accounts of the escape routes of John Wilkes Booth and Jack Ruby were drawn from the general assassination sources cited in Chapter 1.

Chapter 11

The background and fate of Boston Corbett were drawn from the general assassination sources cited in Chapter 1, along with *The Madman and the Assassin: The Strange Life of Boston Corbett, the Man Who Killed John Wilkes Booth* by Scott Martelle (Chicago Review Press, 2015); *Worst Seat in the House: Henry Rathbone's Front Row View of the Lincoln Assassination* by Caleb Jenner Stephens (Willow Manor Publishing, 2014); *Abraham Lincoln and Boston Corbett, with Personal Reflections of Each; John Wilkes Booth and Jefferson Davis: A True Story of Their Capture* by Byron Berkley Johnson (Kessinger Publishing, 1914) as well as the New England Historical Society's website (newenglandhistoricalsociety.com), the Library of Congress website (loc.gov), the Kansas Historical Society website (kshs.org), an April 12, 2015, *Washingtonian* article ("The Insane Story of the Guy Who Killed the Guy Who Killed Lincoln" by Bill Jensen), and an article in the June/July 1980 issue of *American Heritage* ("American Characters: Boston Corbett" by Richard F. Snow). The background of Jack Ruby was drawn from the general assassination sources cited in Chapter 1, with details about the film *Ruby* culled from nytimes.com and imdb.com.

Chapter 12

Details about the more metaphysical aspects of the connections were drawn from *Haunted America* by Michael Norman & Beth Scott (Tor Books, 2007); *My Turn: The Memoirs of Nancy Reagan* by Nancy Reagan with William Novak (Random House, 1989); a December 19, 2017, article in *Psychology Today* ("Synchronicities: A Sure Sign You're on the Right Path" by Gregg Levoy); and an October 31, 2017, article in *Forbes* ("The Mandela Effect—Bad Memories or an Alternate Universe?"), along with *Demon Magazine* (hcs.harvard.edu/~demon), historynet.com, history.com, people.howstuffworks.com, ghost-story.co.uk, astrologyresearch.co.uk, washingtonpost.com, mentalfloss.com, clickhole.com, livescience.com, and news.avclub.com.

Bibliography

Interviews

Matt Anderson
David Byers
Stephen Fagin

April Foran
Jim Gardner
Harry Rubenstein

Charles Sable
Alan Weiss

Books

Anderson, Brian, for Ford's Theatre Society. *Images of America: Ford's Theatre*. Charleston, SC: Arcadia, 2014.

Bishop, Jim. *The Day Kennedy Was Shot*. New York: HarperCollins, 1968.

Bishop, Jim. *The Day Lincoln Was Shot*. New York: Gramercy Books, 1955.

Bogart, Thomas A. *Backstage at the Lincoln Assassination*. Washington, D.C.: Regnery History, 2013.

Boyd, John W., M.D. *Images of America: Parkland Hospital*. Charleston, SC: Arcadia, 2015.

Bugliosi, Vincent. *Reclaiming History: The Assassination of John F. Kennedy*. New York: W.W. Norton, 2007

Collins, Gail. *William Henry Harrison*. New York: Henry Holt, 2012.

Connally, John, with Mickey Herskowitz. *In History's Shadow: An American Odyssey*. New York: Hyperion, 1993.

Doty, Mark, and John H. Slate. *Images of America: John F. Kennedy Sites in Dallas-Fort Worth*. Charleston, SC: Arcadia, 2013.

Eckert, Allan W. *A Sorrow in Our Heart: The Life of Tecumseh*. New York: Bantam Books, 1992.

Eckert, Allan W. *Tecumseh! A Play*. Boston: Little, Brown, 1974.

Fagin, Stephen. *Assassination and Commemoration: JFK, Dallas, and The Sixth Floor Museum at Dealey Plaza*. Norman: University of Oklahoma Press, 2013.

Gardner, Martin. *The Magic Numbers of Dr. Matrix*. Buffalo: Prometheus Books, 1985

Gardner, Martin. *Undiluted Hocus-Pocus: The Autobiography of Martin Gardner*. Princeton: Princeton University Press, 2013.

Johnson, Byron Berkley. *Abraham Lincoln and Boston Corbett, With Personal Reflections of Each; John Wilkes Booth and Jefferson Davis: A True Story of Their Capture*. Waltham: Kessinger, 1914.

Jones, Louis Clark. *Things That Go Bump in the Night*. Syracuse: Syracuse University Press, 1983.

Jortner, Adam. *The Gods of Prophetstown: The Battle of Tippecanoe and the Holy War for the American Frontier*. Oxford: Oxford University Press, 2012.

Lattimer, Dr. John K. *Kennedy and Lincoln: Medical & Ballistic Comparisons of Their Assassinations*. New York: Harcourt Brace Jovanovich, 1980.

Mallon, Thomas. *Henry and Clara*. New York: Vintage, 1994.

Martelle, Scott. *The Madman and the Assassin: The Strange Life of Boston Corbett, the Man Who Killed John Wilkes Booth.* Chicago: Chicago Review Press, 2015.

The Newseum, with Cathy Trost and Susan Bennett. *President Kennedy Has Been Shot.* Naperville: Sourcebooks Media Fusion, 2003.

Norman, Michael, and Beth Scott. *Haunted America.* New York: Tor Books, 2007.

Posner, Gerald. *Case Closed: Lee Harvey Oswald and the Assassination of JFK.* New York: Anchor Books, 1993.

Reagan, Nancy, with William Novak. *My Turn: The Memoirs of Nancy Reagan.* New York: Random House, 1989.

Reston, James, Jr. *The Lone Star: The Life of John Connally.* New York: Harper & Row, 1989.

Slate, John, and Willis C. Winters. *Images of America: Dealey Plaza.* Charleston, SC: Arcadia, 2013.

Stashower, Daniel. *The Hour of Peril: The Secret Plot to Murder Lincoln Before the Civil War.* New York: Minotaur Books, 2013.

Steers, Edward, Jr. *Blood on the Moon: The Assassination of Abraham Lincoln.* Lexington: University Press of Kentucky, 2001.

Stephens, Caleb Jenner. *Worst Seat in the House: Henry Rathbone's Front Row View of the Lincoln Assassination.* Fredericksburg: Willow Manor, 2014.

Sugden, John. *Tecumseh: A Life.* New York: Henry Holt, 1997.

Swanson, James. *Bloody Crimes: The Funeral of Abraham Lincoln and the Chase for Jefferson Davis.* New York: Harper Perennial, 2010.

Swanson, James. *End of Days: The Assassination of John F. Kennedy.* New York: William Morrow, 2013.

Swanson, James. *Manhunt: The 12-Day Chase for Lincoln's Killer.* New York: Harper Perennial, 2006.

Warren Commission. *The Official Warren Commission Report on the Assassination of President John F. Kennedy.* Garden City: Doubleday, 1964.

Periodicals

American Heritage
America's Civil War Magazine
Cincinnati Daily Gazette
Dallas News
Dallas Observer
Dayton Daily News
Demon Magazine
Findlay Morning Republican
Kansas City Star
Los Angeles Times
Magazine of American History
The New Yorker

Newsweek
Parkland Hospital Highlights
Popular Mechanics
Psychology Today
Rock Island Dispatch–Argus
Skeptical Inquirer
Smithsonian Magazine
Texas Monthly
Time
Washingtonian
Weekly View

Websites

abrahamlincolnonline.org
astrologyresearch.co.uk
avclub.com
bbc.com
blog.newspapers.library.in.gov
boston.com

businessinsider.com
c-span.org
chicagotribune.com
clickhole.com
fords.org
fox2detroit.com

ghost-story.co.uk
histdocs.com
history.com
historynet.com
historyonthenet.com
houstonpress.com
imdb.com
indianapublicmedia.org
jfk.hood.edu
jfk.org
kshs.org
lincolncollection.tumblr.com
lincolnconspirators.com
livescience.com
loc.gov
martin-gardner.org
mentalfloss.com
mlive.com
newenglandhistoricalsociety.com
news.newspapers.com
nps.gov
nydailynews.com
nytimes.com
ohiohistorycentral.org

oldcarsweekly.com
parklandhospital.com
people.howstuffworks.com
rogerebert.com
sangamoncountyhistory.org
scientificamerican.com
smithsonianmag.com
snopes.com
spaghetti-western.net
tcm.com
thedailybeast.com
thehenryford.com
thenationalnews.com
thoughtco.com
tshaonline.org
tsl.texas.gov
twincities.com
upi.com
usatoday.com
washingtonpost.com
weta.org
wfmu.org
youtube.com

Index